Charles Fraser Mackintosh

An Account of the Confederation of Clan Chattan; its Kith and Kin

Charles Fraser Mackintosh

An Account of the Confederation of Clan Chattan; its Kith and Kin

ISBN/EAN: 9783337182274

Printed in Europe, USA, Canada, Australia, Japan

Cover: Foto ©ninafisch / pixelio.de

More available books at **www.hansebooks.com**

MINOR SEPTS OF CLAN CHATTAN.

MACKINTOSH.

AN ACCOUNT

OF

THE CONFEDERATION OF

CLAN CHATTAN;

ITS KITH AND KIN.

PREPARED AT THE REQUEST OF THE CLAN ASSOCIATION
IN GLASGOW.

BY

CHARLES FRASER-MACKINTOSH,
OF DRUMMOND, LL.D., F.S.A., SCOT.

GLASGOW: JOHN MACKAY, "CELTIC MONTHLY" OFFICE,
9 BLYTHSWOOD DRIVE.

1898.

PREFACE.

THIS book has been undertaken by request of the active and zealous Clan Chattan Association in Glasgow, who, having given the name, accept the responsibility, and therefore relieve me from the animadversions of some critics, who object to the term "Minor" Septs of Clan Chattan.

Thus, though not bound to defend the name assigned, it is at least incumbent to say that no slur was, is, or can be intended. While the Clan Chattan had its head and leader, to whom all the members gave obedience when it met as a whole; yet composed as it was of various tribes, with different surnames, it resulted that each tribe had its Chieftain, supreme over his own tribe, but subsidiary to the Captain, as a matter of prudence and policy. Clanship was necessarily, in its original form, elective and voluntary. If, after experience, the clan flourished under its elected Chief, there was naturally a disinclination to break off from the victorious leader, or his successors. Discussions, differences, and internal dissensions, more or less, became in time unavoidable, such dissensions being always fostered by jealous neighbours. Clan Chattan from and after 1292 flourished, and became such a power as to excite the determined and hereditary hostility of the Gordons, themselves Southern interlopers. Murdering one Chief, inciting the members of the clan to throw off their allegiance, so as to aggrandize themselves, initiating troubles which have lasted to the present day, such were their nefarious objects. These designs, after some success, were frustrated for a time by the determination of William Mackintosh, first of Borlum, to whom credit must be given for negotiating the great Bond of Union among the Clan Chattan in 1609, of which a *fac-simile* is for the first time printed. This was the second Bond of Union, but alas! the first Bond, granted in 1397, after the battle on the North Inch of Perth, has for some time been missing. The second Bond, which was given in 1664, brings in the Farquharsons; while that of 1756 shows the composition of the clan after the slaughter of Culloden, and after clanship was abolished.

One word as to Tartans. Upon this subject I am no authority, and as some valued correspondents were against the inclusion, I hesitated. On the other hand, there seemed a preponderance in favour, and they are included, taken in some cases from old and valued sources. My friend, Mr. Mackintosh Mackintosh, to whom I am so much indebted, in particular, though by birth a Shaw, is very clear that the Shaw Tartan is not authentic; and that there was only one real Tartan, that of Mackintosh.

May I suggest to those more immediately concerned, that as the Chieftain of the Macphails has through these papers turned up in Australia, other septs, such as the Macbeans, etc., should see to it, and re-establish their proper distinctive position. They will be heartily welcomed.

As to the Macphersons, I have not included them, because they probably would be offended if placed among the tribes as dealt with, while on the other hand, it would be inconsistent with truth to place them otherwise.

This first attempt to deal with a particular branch of very ancient history must be accepted with all its shortcomings, though I trust few errors. A beginning has been made, to be followed, it is hoped, by much new and interesting matter.

My best acknowledgments are due to Mr. Drummond Norie of Glasgow, and Messrs. Watson and Senior of Inverness, for their special illustrations; to many friends, such as Mr. Alex. Macbain, M.A., of Inverness, who have furnished me with information; and to Mr. John Mackay, the publisher, for the really handsome manner in which the book has been issued to subscribers.

C. FRASER-MACKINTOSH.

INVERNESS, *June*, 1898.

CONTENTS.

Preface,	v.
Contents,	vii.
List of Illustrations,	ix.
List of Tartans,	xi.
List of Clan Bonds,	xi.
List of Subscribers,	xiii.
I.—The MacGillivrays.	1
II.—The Macbeans,	30
The Macbeans of Drummond, and others in the Parish of Dores,	36
The Macbeans of Faillie,	42
The Macbeans of Tomatin, etc.,	49
III.—The Macphails of Inverairnie,	57
IV.—The Macqueens,	63
The Macqueens of Pollochaig, Clune, and Strathnoon,	77
V.—The Shaws of Rothiemurchus,	83
The Shaws of Tordarroch,	89
The Shaws of Dell,	97
The Shaws of Dalnavert,	101
The Shaws, or M'Ays, of the Black Isle,	103
The Shaws of Aberdeen, Perth and the Isles,	104
VI.—The Clarks,	112
VII.—The Gows,	118
VIII.—The Davidsons, or Clan Dhai,	123

CONTENTS.

IX.—The Macleans of the North (Clan Thearlaich),	129
X.—The Macintyres of Badenoch (Clan an t-Saoir),	136
XI.—The Clan Tarrill,	139
XII.—The Clan Gillandrish—Macandrews,	142
XIII. Vic Gories,	144
XIV.—Clan Dhu of Strathnairn,	145
XV.—Sliochd Gillie vor Mac Aonas,	145
XVI. Clan Finlay Cheir,	146
XVII.—The Farquharsons, or Clan Fionlay,	147
The Farquharsons of Invercauld,	147
The Farquharsons of Inverie,	161
The Farquharsons of Monaltrie,	162
The Farquharsons of Whitehouse,	163
The Farquharsons of Haughton,	167
The Farquharsons of Allargue and Breda,	169
The Farquharsons of Finzean,	170
XVIII. The "Kith and Kin" of Clan Chattan,	173
Cattanach,	173
Crerar,	173
Gillespie,	173
Gillies,	173
Noble,	174
MacHardies,	174
MacOmie,	175
Mackintoshes of Dalmunzie,	177
Toshes, or Toshachs, and MacGlashans,	179

APPENDIX.

I. Macbeans,	181
II. Macphails,	182
III. Macqueens,	183

CONTENTS.

IV. Shaws,		183
V. Clarks,		184
VI.—MacIntyres,		185
VII.—MacAndrews,		185
VIII.—Davidsons,		186

ILLUSTRATIONS.

The MacGillivrays—Coat of Arms,	1
MacGillivray, from M'Ian's "Clans,"	3
The Stone of the Swords,	14
MacGillivray's Well, and Monument on Culloden Field,	16
MacGillivray's Well, Culloden Field,	27
J. W. MacGillivray, Chieftain of the MacGillivrays,	29
Kinchyle House, Inverness-shire,	32
Gillies Macbean defending the Dyke at Culloden,	35
Fac simile of Signatures to Macbean Deed of 1721,	38
Faillie House, Daviot, Inverness-shire,	43
Faillie Bridge, Daviot, Inverness-shire,	47
The Macbeans of Tomatin—Coat of Arms,	49
The Findhorn Viaduct at Tomatin,	50
Tomatin House, Inverness-shire,	53
The Macphails of Inverairnie—Coat of Arms,	57
The Macqueens—Coat of Arms,	63
Corrybrough House,	64
Fac simile of Receipt by Donald Fraser to the Chief of Mackintosh, 1744,	71
Anvil of Donald Fraser, "Captain of the Five,"	72
Donald Macqueen of Corrybrough, present chieftain,	76
Sword of Donald Fraser, Hero of the Rout of Moy,	79
Tombstone of Donald Fraser, in Moy Churchyard,	80
The Shaws of Rothiemurchus—Coat of Arms,	83
Standing Stones upon Modern Tombstone over the Grave of Shaw Mackintosh of Rothiemurchus,	85
Loch-an-Eilean Castle—the Ancient Stronghold of the Shaws of Rothiemurchus,	88

CONTENTS.

The Shaws of Tordarroch—Coat of Arms,	89
Tordarroch House (modern),	90
Tordarroch Bridge,	92
Major-General John Shaw, of the Tordarroch family,	94
Newhall, Ross-shire—Seat of Charles F. H. Shaw-Mackenzie,	95
Charles F. H. Shaw-Mackenzie, present chieftain of the Shaws of Tordarroch,	96
Fac-simile of Signature of the Rev. Lachlan Shaw, the Historian,	99
Fac-simile of Crathinard's License,	106
Prince Charlie Relics, used in his wanderings, in possession of Major D. Shaw, Inverness, viz:—(1) Portrait of Prince Charlie; (2) Medallion of Marie Clementina Sobieski; (3) Obverse of the Sobieski Medallion,	108-109
The Clarks—Coat of Arms,	112
The Gows—Coat of Arms,	118
Historical Relics in the possession of Mackintosh of Mackintosh, Moy Hall,	120
Arms of Davidson of Cantray,	123
Davidson, from M'Ian's "Clans,"	124
Macleans of Dochgarroch—Coat of Arms,	129
Castle Spiridan, Bona Ferry, Stratherrick Hills, and Loch Ness,	130
Old House of Dochgarroch,	134
The Farquharsons—Coat of Arms,	147
Farquharson, from M'Ian's "Clans,"	148
Invercauld House,	151
Anne Farquharson, Lady Mackintosh,	154
Farquharson of Whitehouse—Coat of Arms,	163
Captain Henry Farquharson,	163
Dr. William Farquharson,	163
Patrick Farquharson,	164
Marjory Stewart, wife of Patrick Farquharson,	165
Andrew Farquharson,	166
Whitehouse, Aberdeenshire,	166
R. F. O. Farquharson, of Haughton,	167
Mrs. Farquharson,	167

CONTENTS.

Haughton House,	168
Major-General George Macbain Farquharson, of Breda,	169
Breda House,	170
Dr. Farquharson of Finzean, and Friends,	171
Finzean House,	172

LIST OF TARTANS.

Mackintosh,	*Frontispiece*
Macgillivray,	facing page 1
Macbean,	,, ,, 30
Macqueen,	,, ,, 63
Shaw,	,, ,, 83
Davidson,	,, ,, 123
Macintyre,	,, ,, 136
Farquharson,	,, ,, 147

LIST OF CLAN BONDS.

1.—*Fac-simile* Bond by and amongst the Clan Chattan, 1609,   Appendix.
2.—*Fac-simile* Bond by and amongst the Clan Chattan, 1664,   ,,
3. *Fac-simile* Deed of Consent by the Clan Chattan, 1756,   ,,

LIST OF SUBSCRIBERS.

Adam, Frank, Esq., Rangoon, Burmah.
Alexander, Captain A. C., Seaforth Highlanders

Bain, James, Esq., Public Library, Toronto, Canada
Barrett, F. T., Esq., The Mitchell Library, Glasgow
Benedict, Curtis C., Esq., Attorney at law, Wis., U.S.A.
Bickers & Son, Messrs, Booksellers, London
Blair, The Late Sheriff, Inverness
Brown, William, Esq., Bookseller, Edinburgh (3 copies)
Brooks, Sir William Cunliffe, Bart., Aboyne
Burgess, Captain Alexander, Gairloch
Burgess, Peter, Esq., Fortrose

Cameron, A. H. F., Esq., M.D., Gloucestershire
Campbell, A. D., Esq., J.P., Cape Colony
Campbell, George J., Esq., Sheriff-Substitute of the Lews
Campbell, George Murray, Esq., Surrey
Carnegie, Andrew, Esq., Skibo Castle, Sutherland
Chisholm, Kenneth Mackenzie, Esq., M.D., J.P., Lancs.
Clark, A. Campbell, Esq., M.D., F.F.P.S.G., Hartwood.
Clark, Charles, Esq., Great St. Helens, London
Clark, Daniel, Esq., Lochend Road, Leith
Clark, J. W., Esq., Hall Road, London
Clark, John T., Esq., Rose Street, Aberdeen
Clark, Richard, Esq., Learmonth Terrace, Edinburgh

LIST OF SUBSCRIBERS.

Clark, Stewart, Esq., Paisley
Clark, Colonel William, Commanding 51st and 65th Regimental Districts
Clark, William, Esq., West George Street, Glasgow
Colquhoun, Sir James, Bart., of Luss
Colquhoun, Lady, of Luss
Cowan, George, Esq., Edinburgh
Crerar, Duncan Macgregor, Esq., New York, U.S.A.
Cunynghame, Miss Ethel, London

Davidson, Lieutenant-Colonel Arthur, Equerry to the Queen
Davidson, Ben., Esq., New York, U.S.A.
Davidson, Surgeon-Captain, D.M., Edinburgh
Davidson, George Walter, Esq., Queen's Gate, London
Davidson, Henry C., Esq., Montgomery, Alabama, U.S.A.
Davidson, Colonel J., 8th Hussars, Balnagask
Davidson, James Mackenzie, Esq., M.B., C.M., London
Davidson, James, Esq., Kirriemuir
Davidson, J. Scott, Esq., of Cairnie
Davidson, Miss, Woodcroft, Edinburgh
Davidson, Samuel, Esq., Dunfermline
Davidson, S. C., Esq., Bangor, Ireland
Davidson, Thomas, Esq., Essex Co., New York, U.S.A.
Davidson, Thomas, Esq., West Hampstead, London
Davidson, W. E., Esq., C.B., Q.C., London
Davidson, William George, Esq., Hon. Secy., Clan Chattan Assoc., Glasgow
Davidson, Duncan, Esq., of Tulloch
Douglas and Foulis, Messrs., Booksellers, Edinburgh (3 copies)

Farquharson, Francis, Esq., of Belnabodach
Farquharson, George, Esq., of Whitehouse
Farquharson, Major-General George MacBain, of Breda
Farquharson, Mrs., of Haughton, F.R.M.S. (6 copies)

LIST OF SUBSCRIBERS.

Farquharson, John, Esq., Banchory
Farquharson, Robert, Esq., M.D., M.P., Finzean
Fraser, Alexander, Esq., Solicitor, Inverness
Fraser, J. A. Lovat, Esq., M.A., Barrister-at-law, London

Gillespie, Colonel G. L., New York City, U.S.A.
Gillespie, Sir Robert, J.P., D.L., Brighton
Gillies, T. R., Esq., Advocate, Aberdeen
Gow, J., Esq., Brunswick Square, London
Gow, Walter, Esq., Cambuslang
Gray, George, Esq., Clerk of the Peace, Glasgow
Gray-Buchanan, A. W., Esq., Polmont
Grevel & Co., Messrs., Booksellers, London

Holland, Richard D., Esq., of Kilvean, Inverness
Hunter, William Sutherland, Esq., Kildonan, Pollokshields

Inverness Free Public Library.
Irving, Mrs. Bell, Glen Chattan, N.W.T., Canada

Kemball, Lady, Lowndes Square, London

MacAndrew, J., Esq., London
MacAndrew, William, Esq., Colchester
MacAndrew, Captain John Maclean, Dalcross Castle
Macaulay, D. J., Esq., M.D., Halifax
Macbain, Edward B., Esq., Bridge of Weir
Macbain, Norman, Esq., Solicitor, Arbroath
Macbain, William, Esq., New York, U.S.A.
Macbean, Æneas Allison, Esq., Glasgow
Macbean, Major Alexander, Mayor of Wolverhampton
Macbean, Andrew, Esq., Invergordon
Macbean, David, Esq., Parkview Gardens, Glasgow
Macbean, Lieutenant-Colonel Forbes, Dover

LIST OF SUBSCRIBERS.

Macbean, Lachlan, Esq., of Tomatin (4 copies)
Macbean, William M., Esq., New York, U.S.A.
Macbean, Robert Baillie, Esq., Lancaster
Macdonald, A⁰ Esq., M.A., LL.D., Glenarm
Macdonald, I ., Esq., of Dunach
Macdonald, ʼ :oneth, Esq., Town Clerk, Inverness
Macdonald, Lachlan, Esq., of Skeabost
MacEwen, William C., Esq., W.S., Edinburgh (2 copies)
MacFall, Captain Crawford, The K.O.Y. Light Infantry
MacFall, Lieutenant C. Haldane, London
MacGeachy & Co., Messrs. James, Booksellers, Glasgow
Macgillivray, Alexander, Esq., Camden Town, London
Macgillivray, Charles W., Esq., M.D., Edinburgh
Macgillivray, Donald, Esq., Islay
Macgillivray, Hugh F., Esq., Manchester
Macgillivray, J. W., Esq., of Dunmaglass
Macgillivray, P., Esq., Inverkip
Macgillivray, R., Masterton, New Zealand
Macgillivray, W. A., Esq., W.S., Edinburgh
Macgillivray, Messrs. William and M., Barra
Macgregor, D. R., Melbourne, Victoria
Macgregor, George, Esq., London
Macgregor, John, Esq., Bearsden
MacHardy, William, Esq., Solicitor, Edinburgh
MacIntosh, Andrew, Esq., Inverness
MacIntosh, John F., Esq., Crosshill, Glasgow
MacIntosh, William, Esq., J.P., Drummuir
MacIntyre, Peter, Esq., Gwydyr Ugha, N. Wales
MacIntyre, J.P., Esq., London
Mackay, John, Esq., C.E., J.P., Hereford
Mackay, Thomas, Esq., Largs

LIST OF SUBSCRIBERS.

Mackay, Councillor William, Solicitor, Inverness
Mackay, William, Esq., Bookseller, Inverness
Mackenzie, Colonel Hector, London
Mackenzie, William, Esq., Secretary, Crofters' Commission
Mackenzie, W. Dalziel, Esq., of Farr
Mackinnon, Duncan, Esq., London (2 copies)
Mackinnon, The Late Sir William A., K.C.B.
Mackintosh of Mackintosh, Moy Hall
Mackintosh, Eneas N., Esq., The Doune
Mackintosh, A. Mackintosh, Esq., Geddes House, Nairn
Mackintosh, Andrew, Esq., Bank of New South Wales, Victoria
Mackintosh, Angus, Esq., of Holme
Mackintosh, D., Esq., Stroud Green, London
Mackintosh, Donald, Esq., Roseheath, Inverness
Mackintosh, Donald A. S., Esq., Shettleston
Mackintosh, E. W., Esq., of Raigmore
Mackintosh, Ex-Bailie John, Southwood, Inverness
Mackintosh, John, Esq., Solicitor, 15 Union Street, Inverness
Mackintosh, Superintendent William, Regent Park Square, Glasgow
Maclean, Alexander Scott, Esq., Greenock
Maclean, Lieutenant Hector F., younger of Duart, Scots Guards
Macleod, Neil, Esq., Raasay
Macneill, Nicolas, Esq., Buenos Ayres, South America
Macpherson, Captain J. F., Caledonian United Service Club
Macpherson, Robert Barclay, Esq., New York, U.S.A.
Macphail, R. S. Rutherford, Esq., M.D., Derby
Macphail, Paul, Esq., of Inverairnie, Victoria
Macqueen, Donald, Esq., of Corrybrough
Macqueen, Donald, Esq., Campbeltown
Macqueen, Miss Flora G., Folkestone
Macqueen, James, Esq., of Crofts, Dalbeattie

LIST OF SUBSCRIBERS.

Macqueen, William, Esq., The Cedar, Norwich
MacRae-Gilstrap, Captain John, Newark-on-Trent
Macvean, C. A., Esq., of Kilfinichen, Mull
Menzies, Colonel Duncan, Blarich, Sutherland
Munro, John, Esq., Hanley
Munro, W. C., Esq., Hawke's Bay, New Zealand

Noble, Archibald, Esq., Leith
Noble, Captain Sir Arthur, of Ardmore, K.C.B., D.C.L., F.R.S.
Noble, Donald, Esq., South Kensington, London
Noble, Edward, Esq., Carnarvon, North Wales
Noble, Kenneth D., Esq., Helensburgh

Ramsden, Sir John W., Bart., Ardverikie
Reay, Lord, G.C.S.I., G.C.I.E., LL.D.
Robertson, G. C., Esq., of Widmerpool
Robertson, Wm. John, Esq., The Hollies, Cheshire
Ross, John Macdonald, Esq., Glasgow
Russell, T. H., Esq., Hightown

Serra Largo, The Count de, of Tarlogie
Shaw, Captain A. G., Avon Lodge, Berkshire. (2 copies.)
Shaw, Albert, Esq., Editor, *The Review of Reviews*, New York, U.S.A.
Shaw, Charles Bousfield, Esq., St. James' Square, London
Shaw, Captain D. A. L., 1st Punjab Cavalry
Shaw, Lieut-General David, London
Shaw, Duncan, Esq., W. S., Inverness
Shaw, Colonel E. W., Eastbourne
Shaw, Lieut-Colonel F. G., J.P., Heathburn Hall, Co. Cork
Shaw, James, Esq., M.D., Waddesdon
Shaw, James Walter, Esq., New York, U.S.A.
Shaw, John, Esq., S.S.C., Edinburgh

LIST OF SUBSCRIBERS.

Shaw, Mackenzie S., Esq., Mount Blair, Glenshee
Shaw, Marshall F., Esq., New York, U.S.A.
Shaw, Rodney K., Esq., Marietta, U.S.A.
Shaw, S. Hamilton, Esq., M.D., Liverpool
Shaw, Thomas, Esq., Q.C., M.P., Edinburgh
Shaw, Walter, Esq., London
Shaw-Mackenzie, Charles F. H., Esq., of Newhall
Shaw-Mackenzie, John A., Esq., M.D., London
Sopper, William, Esq., of Dunmaglass
Sutherland, Charles J., Esq., M.D., South Shields

Wight & Co., Messrs. John, Tartan Warehousemen, 105 Princes Street, Edinburgh
Wright, C. F. Hagberg, Esq., Secretary, London Library

Yule, Miss Amy F., Tarradale

MACGILLIVRAY.

MINOR SEPTS OF CLAN CHATTAN.

THE MACGILLIVRAYS.

OF old the Clan Chattan were reckoned under two classes, the first sprung of the Chief's own house, and the second those who had incorporated or attached themselves, though of other names than that of Mackintosh. Amongst the latter class the MacGillivrays stood the first and oldest, for according to the Croy MS. history, compiled by the Rev. Andrew Macphail, who it is understood died minister of Boleskine, 1608, it is said that about the year 1268 "Gillivray, the progenitor of the Clan vic Gillivray, took protection and dependence for himself and posterity of this Farquhard Mackintosh (5th of Mackintosh, who was killed in 1274, aged 36)."

A

Sir Eneas Mackintosh in his manuscript, privately printed in 1892 by the present Chief, and 28th of Mackintosh, gives the date as 1271.

The origin of the name may be looked for in the last part of MacGillivray, for invariably in Gaelic, and in my younger days, elderly people in good position placed the accent on this last portion, and not as is now invariably done in English, on the second.

Betwixt the first, and Duncan (whom I place as 1st of Dunmaglass) who lived about 1500, is a long step, and it is not the purpose of these papers to do other as a rule, than deal with facts.

It may be taken for granted that the MacGillivrays came from the west, but have been settled at Dunmaglass, in the braes of Strathnairn, and along the valley of Nairn, long before we know their authentic history. In the year 1791, one, Farquhar M'Gillivour, aged 82, living on the banks of the river Nairn, was examined in court, and in answer to a query what his real name was, said he was called Farquhar M'Gillivour in every part of the country, and that the M'Gillivours were followers of the MacGillivrays, having come at the same time from the Western Islands. The descent of the Dunmaglass family was reckoned very high in the Highlands; and the late John Lachlan the 10th, who was exceedingly proud, and in his latter days a very reserved man, used in his cups to declare "he was descended of Kings."

Dunmaglass, at least one half of it, belonged to the old Thanes of Kalder, and is first mentioned in the service of Donald as heir to his father, Andrew, in the lands in the year 1414. The other half belonged to a family named Menzies

From R. Ronald M'Ian's] ("Clans of the Scottish Highlands."
MACGILLIVRAY.

in Aberdeenshire, who in 1419 agreed to sell them to the above Donald Kalder, who in 1421 gets a disposition thereof, described as lying within the barony of Kerdale. Kerdale was one of the extensive baronies belonging to the old estates and Earldom of Moray, but the estate having been broken up, the barony has been long in desuetude. The estate of Dunmaglass, now in one, was of considerable value, being rated as a four pound land of old extent, equivalent to two freeholds.

There is evidence of a Farquhar-vic-Conchie styled of Dunmaglass in the year 1547. I purpose beginning with his father.

I.—Duncan MacGillivray, born probably about 1500—his son,

II.—Farquhar, found in 1547—his son.

III.—Allister Mor, designated as "Allister-vic-Farquhar-vic-Conchie of Dunmaglass," is found on 28th May, 1578, having some connection with a William-vic-Farquhar, and Maggie Kar, spouse of Provost William Cuthbert of Inverness.

By 1609, when the great bond of union among the Clan Chattan was signed, Allister was dead and his son Farquhar being a minor, those who signed for the Clan-vic-Gillivray were Malcolm-vic-Bean in Dalcrombie, Ewen-vic-Ewen in Aberchalder, and Duncan-vic-Farquhar in Dunmaglass. It would also seem that the clan was at this time pretty numerous and influential, and the leader Malcolm, son of Bean MacGillivray in Dalcrombie. In 1593 mention is made of Duncan MacGillivray in Dunmaglass.

IV.—Farquhar. By the year 1620, and probably at a much earlier period, Dunmaglass had been wadsetted by the family of Calder to the MacGillivrays for 1000 merks. In that year Calder was much pinched, and upon Dunmaglass was to be raised other 2000 merks, or to be sold for 5000 merks.

The first alternative was adopted, 2000 merks being eiked in 1622, but the pecuniary pressure still continuing, the estate was feued to Dunmaglass.

It may here be noted, though lying in the centre almost of Inverness-shire, these lands were by an arbitrary exercise of power by the Scottish Parliament, annexed, at Calder's instance, to the County of Nairn.

By feu contract dated at Inverness, 4th April, 1626, John Campbell, Fiar of Calder, with consent of Sir John Campbell, life renter of Calder, his father, feued to Farquhar MackAllister of Downmaglasch, his heirs male and assignees whomsoever— "All and singular the lands and towns of Downmaglasch, extending to a four pound land of old extent, with the mill, multures, mill lands, and sequels of the same, together with houses, biggings, tofts, crofts, woods, fishings, sheallings, grazings, parts, pendicles and pertinents thereof, lying within the Barony of Calder and Sheriffdom of Nairn." The feu duty is £16 Scots, with obligation when required to appear and accompany at his own expense the Lairds of Calder in their progress and journey between Calder and Innerlochie, or Ranoch; to assemble in all lawful conventions, armings, and Royal combats; to attend three head baron courts to be held in the Castle of Calder. This destination to heirs male was kept up, and under it Neil, the 12th laird, succeeded to Dunmaglass.

Dunmaglass, the earliest possession of the family, is a fine estate of some 17,000 acres, with a great mass of table-land on the summit, from whence the waters run eastward to the Findhorn, and westward to the Farigaig. The old mansion house, in which I slept a night after a weary tramp from Dunachton in Badenoch over the Monaliath mountains and across the Cro Clach and the Findhorn rivers, was built towards the close of the seventeenth century, picturesquely situated on a piece of level ground, the western sides dropping rapidly to the river. Since the sale of the property, the old house has been wantonly destroyed.

Farquhar-vic-Allister also acquired the half of the lands of Culclachie from the Earl of Moray, and was infeft 20th December, 1631. He had one sister, Catherine, married to William Mackintosh in Elrig, who is infeft therein 28th September, 1638. I have not observed to whom Farquhar was himself married, but he had a numerous issue, Alexander, Donald, William, Bean, Lachlan, and at least one daughter, Catherine, first married as his second wife to William Mackintosh of Aberarder, in 1653, and afterwards, in 1663, to Martin MacGillivray of Aberchalder. Farquhar's eldest son, Alexander, married Agnes Mackintosh, second daughter of William Mackintosh of Kellachie. Farquhar settled on the young couple by charter, dated Invernes, 27th June, 1643, the two wester ploughs of Dunmaglass.

The Forbeses of Culloden did not find Allister a good neighbour at Culclachie, for by bond registered 24th June, 1654, Kellachie binds himself as cautioner in a law burrows that Allister will keep the peace towards Duncan Forbes of Culloden, John, fiar thereof, and their tenants.

Allister died young, and his widow married in 1657 William Forbes of Skellater.

Farquhar's second son, Donald, commonly called "the Tutor of Dunmaglass," married Marie Mackintosh, and was founder of the Dalcrombie and Letterchullin family, and his descendant in the fifth degree, Neil, ultimately succeeded to Dunmaglass. The MacGillivrays of Dalcrombie long held a good position in Inverness-shire, the last owner, Farquhar, having been at Culloden, but fortunately escaped. All the MacGillivrays were staunch Episcopalians, and Bishop Forbes frequently mentions his warm reception and hospitable treatment when on his periodical visits. Farquhar's relict, Mary, married in 1677 Alexander Mackintosh of Easter Urquhill.

William, the third son of Farquhar, married Mary Macbean and settled in Lairgs, and was great grandfather of the Rev. Lachlan MacGillivray, who was the unsuccessful competitor for the Dunmaglass estates, destined to heirs male, 40 years ago. In 1644 there were three MacGillivrays heritors in Daviot and Dunlichity, viz :—Allister-vic-Farquhar, Malcolm-vic-Bean, and Duncan MacGillivray, and in the time of this Farquhar the MacGillivrays were perhaps at the height of their power, he himself having a deal of property, his sons, Donald and William, establishing a good footing for themselves, and his kinsman at Easter Aberchalder representing an old branch of the house. Not much is known of his sons, Bean and Lachlan, further than that Bean left a son, John, and a reputation not yet forgotten, of being a good fighting man, badly wounded and mutilated in one of the numerous Clan Chattan expeditions to Lochaber. Farquhar generally signed not MacGillivray but "Makallister," of which he seemed proud.

Farquhar appears also to have got in the year 1654 assignation of a heritable tack of the two plough lands of Wester Lairgs and Easter Gask, in Strathnairn, by James, Earl of

Moray, to Hector Mackintosh in 1632, with the usual obligation from the Earl to grant a feu charter when he could; but in consequence of the quarrels and ill feeling betwixt the Morays, and the Cawdors the over superiors holding of the Crown, it was not until after the battle of Culloden and the passing of the Jurisdictions Acts, that the Moray Strathnairn heritable tacksmen got their holdings converted into feu, without Lord Moray incurring the danger of Recognition.

Farquhar and his two sons, Dalcrombie and Lairgs, sign the Clan Chattan Bond of 1664, which as an important historic document, is now given. It is signed by twenty-eight gentlemen, heads of families, including nine Macphersons, five Mackintoshes, four Farquharsons, three MacGillivrays, two MacBeans, two Shaws, one Macqueen, and two others by initials.

"Wee under subscryt, Gentlemen of the name of Clan Chattan, in obedience to His Majesty's authority, and Letters of concurrence granted by the Lords of His Majesty's Privie Council in favour of Lachlan Mackintoshie of Torcastle, our Chieffe, against Evan Cameron of Lochyield, and certain others of the name of Clan Cameron, and for the love and favour we beare to the said Lauchlan, do hereby faithfully promitt and engage ourselves everie one of us for himself, and those under his power, in case the prementional Evan Cameron and those of his kin, now rebells, do not agree with the said Lauchlan anent their present differs and controversies before the third day of February next ensuing, that then and in that case, we shall immediately thereafter upon the said Lauchlan his call, rise with, fortify, concurr and assist the said Lauchlan in the prosecution of the commission granted against the said Evan, to the uttermost of our power, with all those of our respective friends, followers, and defenders, whom we may stopp or lett, or who will anyway be counselled and advised by us to that effect. Now thereto we faithfully engage ourselves upon our reputation and credite and the faith and truth in our bodies, by these subscribed at Kincairne the nineteent day of November and year of God, Sixteen Hundred, Sextie and Four Years."

Farquhar died about 1678. His eldest son, Allister, died young, and by law the active management of affairs fell to the uncle, Donald (though the grandfather was alive), so well known as the Tutor, a man of considerable talent and business capacity. The date of Alexander's death is uncertain, but before 1658, and besides his son and successor, he had, at least, one daughter, Margaret, who married in 1670, William Fraser, apparent of Meikle Garth.

VI.—Farquhar, only son of Allister, is first noticed in March, 1658, when he gets a precept in the half of Culclachie from Alexander, Earl of Moray, as heir to his father, Alexander, sometime fiar of Dunmaglass. On his marriage in 1681 with Emilia Stewart of Newtonne, he settles a jointure on her, furth of Wester Lairgs, Easter Gask, and Easter Culclachie. By this lady, who seems to have been shrewd and sensible (her letters to Inverness merchants, sometimes from Dunmaglass, sometimes from Gask, always stipulate "a good penny worth"), Dunmaglass had a numerous family. Farquhar, who succeeded, Captain William, Donald, Janet, Magdalene, and Anna, all married. This Dunmaglass sold the half of Culclachie, and died early in 1714, his widow surviving until about 1730.

In 1685 Farquhar is named a Commissioner of Supply by Act of Parliament, and the district continued so disturbed after the Revolution, that in 1691 Sir Hugh Campbell of Cawdor recommended a hundred soldiers to be stationed for a time at Dunmaglass as "ane convenient centre." It was in the time of this Farquhar, styled "Fiadhaich," as he was of haughty and turbulent disposition, that the question of marches at Lairgs with the Mackintosh arose, when a witness who swore falsely for Dunmaglass, convicted of perjury on the spot, was buried alive, the place of burial being still pointed out.

Captain William, the second son, married Janet Mackintosh, daughter of Angus Mackintosh of Kellachie, contract dated 9th February, 1714, and had a son, Lachlan of Georgia, commonly called Lachlan "liath," afterwards noticed, also a daughter, Jean "Roy," whose descendants succeeded to Faillie, Invererine, and Wester Gask. David, or Donald, married Miss MacGillivray, of Mid Leys, and was father of Alexander MacGillivray of Ballintruan, whose male issue are extinct. Of Farquhar's three daughters, Janet became Mrs. Donald MacGillivray of Dalcrombie, whose husband was killed near Leys on the afternoon of the 16th April, 1746. Magdalen, afterwards Mrs. Mackintosh of Holm; and Anne, Mrs Fraser of Farraline. Of this Captain William Ban, who died in 1734, the following anecdote is recorded by the late Mr. Simon F. Mackintosh of Farr, under date 1835, in his valuable collections.

A FAIRY TALE—THE CAPTAIN BAN.

"About the beginning of the 18th century the wife of one of the tenants in Druim-a-ghadha, upon the estate of Dunmaglass, had been carried away by the fairies, and was said to to have been taken by them into a small hillock in that neighbourhood, called "Tomnashangan," or the Ants' Hill, and had been absent from her family for nearly a year. No person, however, could tell exactly where she was, although their suspicions fell upon the fairies, and that she must be with them in the hill now mentioned. Several attempts were made to discover her, and none were bold enough to encounter the residence of the fairies. At last Captain William MacGillivray, alias the Captain Ban, (*i.e.* " White "), son of Farquhar MacGillivray of Dunmaglass, who was resident at the spot, at length volunteered his services to endeavour to get the woman released from her long captivity in the " Fairy Hill," if it was possible that she could be there. The Captain being informed that John Dubh (M'Chuile) M'Queen of Pollochaik was familiar and on good terms with the fairies, and that he had wax candles in which there was a particular virtue, he despatched a messenger, who got particular instructions never to look behind him until he reached home, otherwise something might happen to him, and he would lose the candle. This person heard so much noise like that of horses and carriages, accompanied with music and loud cries of 'catch him, catch him' at Craigannain, near Moy Hall, that he was so frightened that he could not help looking behind him, and although he saw nothing, he lost his candle; then he made the best of his way home. A second courier was despatched, who received another candle and the same injunctions. In coming through the same place as the former, he withstood all the noise he heard there, but at a place near Farr, it was ten times worse, and not being able to withstand taking a peep over his shoulder, he lost the object of his message. In this predicament, it became necessary to send a third bearer to Pollochaik for another candle, which he also got, but on coming to the river Findhorn, it was so large that he could not cross, so that he was obliged to go back to the laird of

Pollochaik for his advice, who, upon coming down to the bank of the river, desired the man to throw a stone upon the opposite side of the river, and no sooner was this done than, much to his astonishment, he found himself also there. He then proceeded upon his journey, and having taken a different route across the hills, even here he occasionally heard considerable noise, but he had courage never to look behind him, and accordingly he put the virtued candle into the hands of the Captain Ban.

The Captain being now possessed of Pollochaik's wax candle, he one evening approached the hillock, and having discovered where the entry was, he entered the passage to the fairy habitation, and passing a press in the entrance, it is said that the candle immediately lighted of its own accord, and he discovered that the good lady, the object of his mission, was busily engaged in a reel, and upon obtaining the open air, he told her how unhappy her husband and friends were at the length of time she had been absent from them, but the woman had been so enchanted and enraptured with the society she had been in that she seemed to think she had been only absent one night, instead of a year, from her own house. When the Captain brought her off with him the fairies were so enraged that they said 'they would keep him in view.' The woman was brought to her disconsolate husband, and the candle was faithfully preserved in the family for successive generations in order to keep off all fairies, witches, brownies, and water kelpies in all time to come.

Some time afterwards as the Captain was riding home at night by the west end of Loch Duntelchaig he was attacked and severely beaten by some people he could not recognise. He got home to his own house, but never recovered, and it is said that the mare he rode was worse to him than even those that attacked him, so he ordered her to be shot the next day. He was grand-uncle to the present John Lachlan MacGillivray of Dunmaglass.

The third and successful bearer of the candle was Archibald MacGillivray in   alias "Gillespuig Luath," *i.e.* swift or fast Archibald. He was grand-uncle to Archibald MacGillivray, now tenant in Dunmaglass. Pollochaik said to him that he would have preferred the Captain to have sent for his fold of cattle, than for the candle.

The candle was in possession of some of her descendants about thirty years ago, but was afterwards taken away by some idle boys. The woman lived to such an old age that some of the people still in life remember quite well having seen her shearing the corn upon her knees, in consequence of her having lost the use of the lower limbs."

VII.—Farquhar, eldest son of the above Farquhar, succeeded in 1714, and entered into marriage articles with Elizabeth Mackintosh, daughter of William Mackintosh of Aberarder, upon 8th September, 1716, but the contract is not dated till 8th May, 1717, nor the lady infeft in Dunmaglass, Lairgs, and Gask, until 29th July, 1730, after her mother-in-law's death.

The MacGillivrays took an active part in the rising of 1715. The laird and his brother, William, were Captain and Lieutenant respectively in the Clan Chattan regiment, while there was another Farquhar MacGillivray, also Lieutenant. The two former at least, got off, but one John MacGillivray, apparently of good standing, was tried and convicted on 25th January, and executed at Wigan, 10th February, 1716. This Farquhar was a leading man under Lachlan and William Mackintosh, Chiefs of Clan Chattan, and did much

THE STONE OF THE SWORDS ON WHICH THE MACGILLIVRAYS
AND OTHERS OF CLAN CHATTAN SHARPENED THEIR
SWORDS ON THEIR WAY TO CULLODEN.

to bring about the agreement with the Macphersons in the year 1724. He received from Lachlan Mackintosh a feu of the Davoch of Bochruben in Dores, which he parted with to Fraser of Bochruben, the *dominium utile* ultimately falling into the hands of William Fraser of Balnain, whose posterity still retain it. He was an excellent man of business, but interfering too much with other people's affairs, his own became involved. He died in 1740, but his wife, Elizabeth Mackintosh, is found as late as 1769. He had several children—Alexander, who succeeded; William, who succeeded his brother; John, Farquhar, and Donald, also Anne, Catherine, and Elizabeth. With the exception of William, none left issue.

VIII.—Alexander, the eldest son, succeeded and was extensively engaged, like his uncle, Captain William and other members of his family, in cattle dealing, being known as "Alister-Ruadh-na-Feille." That he was well worthy of the honour of being selected to lead the Clan in 1745-6 is undoubted, and as he lived at Easter Gask the tradition that many of the men who fought at Culloden, sharpened their swords on the singular Druidical standing stone or slab, near Easter Gask, deserves some weight. His gallant conduct on that fatal day, and his death on the field at the Well still bearing his name, is well known. It was part of the cruel system of the conquerors not to allow the bodies of the Highlanders to be carried away for interment by their friends, and consequently they were buried in trenches, whereof the green covering is still to be seen. The ordinary place of sepulture of the Dunmaglass family was and is at Dunlichity, but Dunmaglass' friends feared the publicity of re-interring the remains so far distant, and buried them quietly at Petty. It is recorded in the Farr collection :—

"In the churchyard of Petty lies the Chief of MacGillivrays, who was killed at the Battle of Culloden. After the battle, his body with fifty others was thrown into a large pit, and so far did the King's troops carry their animosity, that for six weeks they guarded the field and would not grant the poor consolation to the friends of men who had fought so well, of placing their mangled carcases in their family burying places. However, at the end of that time, the relations of Dunmaglass dug up the pit where his body had been laid, and when taken up was perfectly fresh, and the wound which was through his heart bled anew. The place they had been thrown into being a moss, is supposed to be the cause of the corpse remaining uncorrupted. The interment was private."

MACGILLIVRAY'S WELL, AND MONUMENT ON CULLODEN FIELD.

Alexander MacGillivray died unmarried, but Mr. Bain of Nairn in his interesting history of Nairnshire, lately published, says he was engaged to Elizabeth Campbell, only child of Duncan Campbell, eldest son of Sir Archibald Campbell of

Clunes, and that they met on the morning of the battle. That they did is hardly likely, though it is said that ladies appeared on the muir on horseback early in the day, but the engagement may be true.

I visited the ruined Chapel of Barevan some years ago, and found Miss Campbell's grave, and by the kindness of a good clansman, Mr. William Mackintosh, farmer at Barevan, received a copy of the inscription, which runs thus:—

"Under this stone are interred the remains of Duncan Campbell of Clunese, and Elizabeth, his only child by Catherine, daughter of John Trotter of Morton Hall, Esq. He died, 23rd January, 1766, aged seventy-five, and she, 22nd August, 1746, aged twenty-four. D. C. E. C."

Supposing the story true, she only survived the death of her betrothed, about four months. Her father, Duncan Campbell, was accessory to the rising of 1715, and had to live abroad for several years, where he married, his wife dying young at Rome. I possess some of Elizabeth's letters, written in a beautiful clear hand, of elegant diction, showing unusual cleverness and dignity in one so young. I give one of them dated 22nd September, 1743, which will be found very interesting, addressed to one of her aunts, who has pinned to the letter this memorandum—"Betty Campbell dyed the 19th August, 1746. Lady Mackintosh (Anna Duff) dyed in the year 1750." Probably the date in the inscription, 22nd August, 1746, refers to her interment. Lord Lovat refers to Elizabeth in a letter to her father—"It is only to serve you and Miss Campbell, your daughter, whose education should now be taken care of, and if she be like her mother, or your mother, she will be an honour to the family of Calder, and to the name of Campbell."

"Dr. Aunt,

As I have been in a sort of a hurry ever since I parted with you, and there was no occasion offered for my writing you, nor had I any thing to say that was of such consequence as was worth while sending a purpose, I hope you'l therefor excuse my neglecting it till now. I am just now busy paying my visits in this country, for as I have fixed the month of October for my going South, I have but little time to lose. My father and I was lately at Kilraick, where we found Lady Geddes bedfast, and was so most part of the time we stayed. I made your compliments and apology to her; we hear that she is now much better. I should be glad your visiting at Castle Downie and Moyhall happened at a time with mine, as I intend being at both places soon, for I must make the best use of my time I can. But if it was never so short I shall endeavour to see you and ask your commands, as it was not only my promise, but is my inclination. When you see Fairfield next, if he talks to you of the subject you spoke to me about when last at Budgate, which I then told you my plain and positive sentiments of (as I did himself before) that you might put a stop as soon as possible, to a thing it was to no purpose to follow, and which I thought was enough to hinder his pursuing or entertaining any thoughts of that kind, nor can I say anything plainer or stronger; without being rude or uncivil; which is what I should be sorry be forced to, as 'tis what I do not incline being to any gentleman; and if he do, let him blame himself for I have done all I can to prevent it; and you may assure him from me that he needs never expect a better answer from me than what he has already got, nor will I ever talk of any particular objections, for that would be entering on a subject that I would scarce know where to begin or end; so that the sooner he gives over any thoughts of that kind, he will certainly find it the better for himself—make my compliments to Duncan and believe me to be,

Dr. Aunt,

Your affe. niece, and humble servt.,

Clunes, Sept. 22nd, 1743."   (Signed)   ELIZ. CAMPBELL.

"This I hope you'l have occasion to call being over cautious (after what I before told you) in stopping what is already ended, but there can be no harm in what I write to you, so you may make what use of it you please."

The MacGillivrays fell in scores at Culloden, including of officers, at least one Colonel, one Major, two Captains, and one Lieutenant.

The mismanagement on the Prince's side was dreadful. Although the Camerons were put on the right, the Macdonalds instead of sulking and allowing themselves to be shot down, ought to have behaved like Malcolm, 10th Mackintosh, at Harlaw. He was much displeased at being displaced from the wonted position of the Clan Chattan on the right, but accepting the position of left, declared he would make the left the real right in course of the action, and did so, fighting with his followers like heroes.

"Wherever Mackintosh sits, *that* is the head of the table."

Then again the poor Mackintoshes were in the centre at Culloden, and kept back, notwithstanding a galling fire, until in desperation they broke forward in fierce charge, too late to be of material service; the enemy well knowing that with Highlanders victory only followed an early and impetuous attack.

IX.—William MacGillivray, a minor, succeeded his brother, Alexander, and to a very embarrassed estate. William Mackintosh, younger of Holm, took charge, and even a new suit of clothes for the boy required grave consideration. He afterwards, through the interest of Lady Mackintosh, got a

Captaincy in the Gordon regiment commanded by Colonel Staats Long-Morris, and though a vassal, was most meanly prevented by the Earl of Moray in 1757 from raising, if he could, recruits out of the Lordships of Petty and Strathdearn. He saw a good deal of service at home and abroad, and was a most kind-hearted man in his family. He got Gask and Lairgs converted into feu holdings, acquired Faillie from Captain Macbean, and the half of Inverairnie, originally part of the Kilravock estate, but occupied for generations by the Macphails. His three brothers, John, Farquhar, and Donald had to make their way in the world, and the two younger died without issue. John, who died at sea in the end of 1778, amassed a considerable fortune, which ultimately fell to John the 10th, and set up the family in a strong position. None of the three sisters, Anne, Elizabeth, or Catherine married—the eldest, Anne, managing the involved affairs of her brother and nephew up to her death in June, 1790, with great shrewdness and determination.

From Captain MacGillivray's numerous letters I select two as specimens, both being addressed to Provost John Mackintosh of Inverness.

LONDON, Feby. 1779.

D. Sir,

I wish you joy, nay double joy, both on account of your marriage with my cousin, Miss Mackintosh, Aberarder, and the addition she has made to your family. She was but a child when I left the country, but promised a great deal of sweetness of temper, a very necessary ingredient in the matrimonial state; and I know your own disposition so well, that I cannot hesitate to pronounce you a happy couple. I flattered myself that I would have the pleasure of seeing your happiness, but my fortune seems now to place that at a distance, as I expect to return soon to Georgia, to recover as much of my property as possible. I hope it is by this time in the hands of the King's troops, without which I have no business there, as I am under sentence of death should they catch me. Please to remember me most affectionately to Mrs. Mackintosh, your sisters and brother-in-law, and believe me to be sincerely,

        D. Sir,
      Your friend and humble servt.,
        (Signed) WILL McGILLIVRAY."

"D. Sir,
   Tho' I hear but seldom from your quarter, yet you and all my friends are as near my heart as ever, and every favourable account warms my heart with joy. But the present occasion of my writing you is of a different nature, and tho' expected, distressing, and must be felt like everything of the kind for a length of time. I mean my good sister Katy's death. She deserved well of me, and everybody. Her change must be happy. Her illness and death and the illness of my other sister, Betty, must be attended with expense. I wrote my sister Anny (who must have suffered much on the occasion) some considerable time ago, to draw on me for what they might stand in need of; but as I have had no intimation on that head, I shall be much obliged to you, if you will let my sister Anny have what money she may want, and by the first opportunity acquaint her accordingly. Upon letting me know the amount, I will order your bill to be answered at London.

  Mrs. McGillivray joins in wishing you, and yours, and our friends and acquaintance about the Ness, many merry and happy returns of the season.

     I am, D. Sir,
       Yours sincerely,
        (Signed) WILL McGILLIVRAY.

Captain William died in 1783, leaving two children, John Lachlan, and Barbara Anne, both very young.

  X.—John Lachlan MacGillivray. His affairs, as well as

those of his uncle, John MacGillivray of Georgia, were carefully administered in his minority chiefly by "Lachlan lia," son of Captain Bàn, who had returned and spent his old age chiefly twixt Dunmaglass and Inverness. The great black wood of Faillie was planted, and two further acquisitions of land were made, viz :—Wester Gask from the Macphersons, and Easter Aberchalder, an old possession of the MacGillivrays.

In June, 1800, John's only sister, Barbara, a lady of great beauty, died in Edinburgh, her fortune falling to her brother, who at his majority was possessed not only of a good deal of money, but also of the seven estates of Dunmaglass, Easter Aberchalder, Wester Gask, Easter Gask, Faillie, Wester Lairgs, and half of Inverairnie.

A sum of £39 19s. was laid out in repairing the tomb at Dunlichity after Miss Barbara MacGillivray's death in 1800.

John Lachlan possessed the estate for nearly seventy years (1783-1852), and his rental at his accession was about £225, rising by the year 1803 to £561 14s. 7d., as follows, from seventy-one tenants :—

EASTER ABERCHALDER—(1803).

Robert M'Gillivray, Kenmore,	£4 16 0
Alexander M'Tavish,	4 16 0
David Smith,	4 16 0
Ewen M'Gillivray,	9 12 0
William M'Gillivray, Balnoidan,	3 10 0
Mary M'Gillivray, widow of Donald M'Pherson, or his son,	3 10 0
Finlay M'Lean, Balnoidan,	2 10 0
John MacTavish and William Douglass, Keppoch,	7 0 0
Duncan M'Tavish, Balnalish,	3 10 0

MINOR SEPTS OF CLAN CHATTAN.

Widow Rose, Balnalish, - -	9	0	0
Jno. Mackintosh, Balnacharnish, -	4	0	0
Malcolm M'Gillivray, there, -	4	0	0
Donald M'Gillivray, there, - - -	4	0	0
The Heirs of Miss Annie M'Gillivray for the grass and wintering of the Mains from Whit. 1802 to ditto 1803,	20	0	0
Sum Rent Easter Aberchalder, £85	0	0

DUNMAGLASS.

Robt. Campbell, The Mains, - -	£70	0	0
Jno. M'Gillivray and Jno. Smith, Drummacline,	21	6	0
Jno. Moir M'Gillivray, Balnaguich, - - -	17	7	4½
The Heirs of Donald M'Gillivray, Dalscoilt and Dalnagoup,	21	2	9
Jno. M'Bean and John Mackintosh, Milltown, - -	10	19	6
Wm. Smith, Donald M'Gillivray, Wm. Bean, Croachy,	13	6	0
Wm. Graham, Croft of Croachy, - - -	19	1	0
Donald M'Gillivray, Lag, - -	7	13	0
Dun. M'Gillivray, Drumchline, - - - -	2	4	0
Jno., Duncan, and Wm. M'Gillivray, Achloddan, -	13	10	7
Sum Rent of Dunmaglass, £196	10	2½

HALF OF INVERAIRNIE.

Angus M'Phail, - - - -	£5	7	0
Jno Bain, Dumbreck, - -	4	0	6
W. Mackintosh of Holm, for part of Mains, -	8	8	0
Angus M'Culloch, - - - - -	6	0	0
Mr. M'Intosh of Farr, for grazing of Shalvanach.	5	0	0
Sum Rent of half Inverairnie, £28	15	6

WESTER GASK.

Donald Clunes, - - - -	£4	2	0
Farquhar Smith, - -	4	7	0

John M'Gillivray, -	-	4 7 0
Alexander M'Kenzie, -	-	1 15 0
John M'Phail, -	-	5 0 0
Duncan Shaw, -	-	5 0 0
Wm. Davidson, -	-	6 0 0
Donald Mackenzie, -	-	6 0 0
John Macgregor and John Smith,		6 0 0
Sum Rent of Wester Gask,		£42 11 0

EASTER GASK.

The Heir of Donald Hood for Mains,	-	£31 10 0
Widow Duncan Mackintosh,	-	4 1 6
Alex. M'Gillivray, Shanval,	-	4 6 6
Alex. Smith, Smith,	-	4 0 0
Alex. M'Gillivray, Canlan,	-	1 17 0
Donald M'Kintosh Miller, for part of Faillie, -		7 10 0
Angus M'Bean, Dalvellan,	-	7 0 0
John Shaw,	-	5 7 6
Sum Rent of Easter Gask,		£65 12 6

FAILLIE.

Alex. Fraser, Balnaluick, -	-	£8 8 2½
Colin M'Arthur, Dyster, -	-	4 5 0
Alex. Munro, Mains,	-	28 11 2
Alex. Fraser, Middtoun, -	-	4 7 6
William M'Beath, -	-	7 12 6
Alex. M'Gillivray, Achlaschylie, -	-	9 15 0
Alex. M'Gregor, ,,		5 10 0
William Shaw, -	-	2 18 6
Ewan M'Donald, Torveneach,	-	4 6 6
Wm. M'Gillivray, West-end,	-	1 4 0
Sum Rent of Faillie,		£76 18 4½

LAIRGS.

	£	s.	d.
Alex M'Gillivray, Ballintruan,	8	7	0
Wm. Davidson or Dean,	6	1	8
James Sutherland,	6	19	1
Widow Ann M'Gillivray or Mackintosh,	5	4	3
Donald Calder,	3	0	0
Wm. M'Bean, Meikle Miln,	10	8	0
Don. M'Gillivray, Cabrach,	2	17	0
Lieut. M'Gillivray, Dell of Lairg,	23	10	0
Sum Rent of Lairgs,	£66	7	0

In 1819 the rent from fifty-nine tenants was as follows: – Easter Aberchalder, thirteen tenants, £266 14s. 9¾d.; Dunmaglass, from thirteen tenants, £453 8s. 9d.; Faillie, six tenants, £161 10s. 10d.; Easter Gask, nine tenants, £159 15s. 0d.; Wester Gask, nine tenants, £102 5s. 0d.; Inverairnie, four tenants, £70 3s. 0d.; Wester Lairgs, five tenants, £160 13s. 1½d. Total from fifty-nine tenants, £1372 10s. 6¼d., and it will be kept in view that shooting rents had not begun.

John Lachlan was very wild in his youth, and Sheriff Fraser, Farraline, one of the guardians, had some difficulty in compounding for his pranks at the College of St. Andrew's in 1797.

He purchased a Cornetcy in the 16th Light Dragoons in 1800 for £735, and a Lieutenancy in the same regiment in 1802 for £262 10s., and was very extravagant. Fortunately, he left the army about 1805, when he married Miss Jane Walcott of Inverness, a lady who had much influence with him for good. They lived at Culduthel, Drummond, travelled abroad a good deal, but had no regular residence except Inverness. After his wife's death, Dunmaglass led a somewhat retired life, and many will recollect his fine military carriage, and how well he sat on horseback as he took his daily rides.

His father-in-law, Captain Thomas Walcott, thus refers to him in his holograph will of 1807:—"Item to John MacGillivray: my own desk that I write at, with the old stock buckle that he gave me. Had I anything worth his acceptance, I should out of gratitude have left it to him."

His rental at his death was only £1496 4s. 0d., which included £180 for shootings. This was about the same as in 1819, but the tenants had been reduced from seventy-one in 1803, to fifty-nine in 1819, and in 1852 numbered less than half, or thirty-five.

He died in 1852 possessed of some £40,000 of money, which was destined by will, including a year's rent to all the tenants; also the heritable estates undisposed of, but free and unburdened. A severe competition arose as to all the estates except one, that of Easter Aberchalder, there being no doubt that it fell to the Hon. John MacGillivray, of Upper Canada, heir male of line of Donald, Tutor of Dunmaglass, and eldest surviving son of Farquhar MacGillivray of Dalcrombie. Dunmaglass, Easter Gask, and Wester Lairgs were destined to heirs male, and the contest was betwixt the said John MacGillivray—who dying, his son, Neil John, descendant of Donald the Tutor—on the one part, and the Rev. Lachlan MacGillivray, descendant of William of Lairgs, brother of Donald the Tutor, on the other part; the question being whether Donald or William was the elder, and determined in favour of Neil John.

Faillie, Wester Gask, and Inverairnie were destined to "the heirs and assignees of Clan Chattan," and competed for by the said Neil on the one part, and the descendants of Jean "Roy," sister of Lachlan "Lia" and daughter of Captain William Bàn MacGillivray, all before mentioned, on the other part: the latter contending that being the nearest heirs of John Lachlan, the limitation to being of Clan

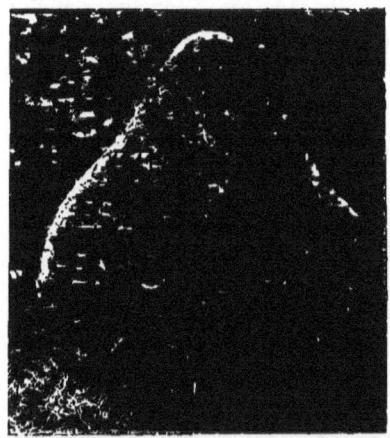

MACGILLIVRAY'S WELL, CULLODEN FIELD.

Chattan had become inoperative. Judgment was given for them, and shortly afterwards these estates were sold.

XI.—The Hon. John succeeded as heir male to John Lachlan in 1852, and died in 1855.

XII.—Neil John, who succeeded his father, John, in Aberchalder, and made good his claims to Dunmaglass, Easter Gask, and Wester Lairgs. He sold the last two estates, and was succeeded in Dunmaglass and Easter Aberchalder by his son

XIII.—J. W. MacGillivray, the present Dunmaglass, in whose time, alas, the remaining estates had to be compulsorily sold, and the whole of the once important estates of the MacGillivrays are lost to the Clan Chattan; except Wester Lairgs, which is the property of The Mackintosh. Though the MacGillivrays are now dissociated from all landed connection with Strathnairn, their memory ought not and is not likely to fade; for Iain-Donn-Mac Shenmais-mhic-Dhaibhidh truly said of the name and race:—

> "Gradh do 'n droing luinneach,
> Mhuirneach, aigeanach ùr
> Aofhuinneach, chliuiteach
> Mhuirnicht' th' aguinn an cùirt
> An fhine nach crion 'sa shiolaidh
> Fad' as gach taobh
> Sàr Bràighich an Dùin
> D' an tug mi mo rùn a chaoidh.
> * * * * * *
> Air chaismeachd luath,
> Thig do chàirdean gu tuath o dheas;
> Fir ghlinne 's glain snuadh,
> Thig á Muile nan stuadh bheann glas,
> Peighinn-a'-Ghàeil le 'sluagh
> Thig thar bhuinne nan cuaintean bras,
> Bidh iad againn 'san uair
> Mu 'm bi mulad no gruaimean ort."

The changes in property and occupation in Inverness-shire within the last fifty years have been very great. Small proprietors have disappeared, and small occupations have been joined to large possessions. No MacGillivray now owns land, and the name has been so scattered, as to be now found in the greatest numbers in clan gatherings and associations within the great cities of the south. MacGillivrays

J. W. MACGILLIVRAY OF DUNMAGLASS, CHIEF OF THE MACGILLIVRAYS.

have a fine record to look back upon, and it is relied on that wherever they are they will act up to it.

The present Dunmaglass is doing well in India, and it is hoped will restore the fortunes of his family.

No. II.—THE MACBEANS.

THIS important tribe of Clan Chattan is coming well to the front, two of its foremost men in Inverness at present being of this name, viz:—the Provost of Inverness, and the Rector of the High School, one of our first Celtic authorities. In the roll of names within the Burgh of Inverness, Macbeans are well represented, and they are found in considerable numbers over the Highlands and the larger Scottish cities. The Macbean territory lay chiefly in the parish of Dores, as may be seen from the preponderance of the name on the tombstones in the churchyard, represented by Kinchyle and Drummond as heritors. They were represented in Strathnairn by Macbean of Faillie, and in Strathdearn by Macbean of Tomatin. Kinchyle was undoubted head, and signs the Bond of Union among the Clan Chattan in 1609; the Bond of Maintenance of 1664; and finally, in 1756, the Letter of Authority from the Clan to Mackintosh, to redeem the Loch Laggan estate. According to the Rev. Lachlan Shaw, the first Macbean came out of Lochaber, in the suit of Eva, heiress of Clan Chattan, and settled near Inverness. The MS. history of the Mackintoshes says in corroboration, that "Bean vic Coil Mor (of whom the Clan Vean had their denomination) lived in Lochaber, and was a faithful servant to Mackintosh against the Red Comyn, who possessed Inverlochie, who was a professed enemy of Mackintosh." Again the manuscript records that Myles Mac-Bean vic-Coil-Mor and his four sons, Paul, Gillies, Myles, and Farquhar, after they

MACBEAN.

had slain the Red Comyn's steward and his two servants, Patten and Kissen, came to William Mackintosh, seventh of Mackintosh (son of Eva), in Connage, in Pettie, where he then dwelt, and for themselves and their posterity took protection and dependence of him and his, as their chief. This occurring about 1334, establishes the Macbeans as one of the oldest tribes of historic Clan Chattan. The Mackintosh history, referring to the battle of Harlaw (1411), narrates that "Mackintosh lost in this battle many of his friends and people, especially of the Clan Vean." This loss so greatly depressed the Macbeans that I am unable to trace the succession from this period until the time of Gillies, about 1500. In 1609, Angus vic Phaol in "Kinchyle, for himself, and taking the full burden in and upon him of his kin and race of the Clan Vean," signs the Bond of Union among the Clan Chattan.

1.—This Angus Macbean received a feu of Kinchyle from Sir John Campbell of Calder, the superior, dated Auldearn, 18th May, 1610. From this Charter in my possession, I observe that Angus is designed "Angus-Mac-Phaol-vic-William-vic-Gillies," whereby we arrive at the names of Angus' father, Paul; grandfather, William; and great-grandfather, Gillies; who may have lived about 1500. Angus Macbean, the first undoubted heritable proprietor of Kinchyle, in the year 1614 added to his estates by the acquisition of the adjoining kirk lands of Durris, called Daars, both properties remaining in the family until the final sale. In 1626, Angus wadsetted from the Earl of Enzie the lands of Bunachton, also in the parish of Dores. Angus left two sons,

KINCHYLE HOUSE, INVERNESS-SHIRE.

II.—John, who made up no title to the estates, and at least one younger son, William, found in 1627. John is designed younger of Kinchyle in 1628, married Mary Macqueen, daughter of Donald Macqueen of Corrybrough, and witnesses a deed connected with the estate of Inverlochie, 31st August, 1619. He appears to have married as his second wife, Isabella Baillie. John was succeeded by his son

III.—Paul, who on 11th May, 1664, receives from Calder, the superior, a precept of Clare Constat, as heir of his grandfather, Angus. Paul, and Annie Urquhart his affianced spouse, daughter of Alexander Urquhart of Kinudie, receive in 1655 a Charter from John Macbean (No. 2 hereof), Angus, another son of John, being one of the witnesses. In 1658 mention is made of John of Kinchyle; of Lachlan Macbean, his brother; and of Paul, as "apparent" of Kinchyle. In 1663, Paul Macbean of Kinchyle; Gillies Macbean in Lagnalian; John and William, brothers to Paul, are mentioned.

Falling into pecuniary troubles, Paul had to relinquish his estates in 1685, when they were re-granted same year by Calder to "William Macbean in Kinchyle," probably son of Paul. This Paul Macbean had one brother, William, and I infer that the well-known Mr. Angus Macbean, Minister of Inverness, was either son or nephew of Paul's.

IV.—William Macbean succeeded Paul; he is infeft on precept from Calder in 1686. Lachlan, his brother german; Angus, Writer, Inverness; and John Macbean, N.P., are among the witnesses. In 1703, there is note of Angus and Donald, lawful sons of William Macbean, younger of Kinchyle.

E

Lachlan Macbean in Kinchyle is Attorney at the taking of William's infeftment, with Gillies Macbean in Wester Draikies and Alexander Macbean, lawful son to Paul Macbean of Kinchyle, as witnesses.

William married, 23rd December, 1688, Jean, second daughter of Donald Mackintosh of Kellachie, and left at least two sons: Eneas, who succeeded, and Gillies. One of the daughters married Alexander Grant, and were the parents of Charles Grant, and grand-parents of Lord Glenelg and Sir Robert Grant. Another daughter, described as Elspet, William's third daughter, married, in 1716, John Macbean of Drummond.

V.—Eneas, the eldest son, married, 1711, Isobel Mackenzie, daughter of Roderick Mackenzie of Redcastle. A post-nuptial contract was entered into in 1718, having the name of Gillies Macbean, brother of Eneas, as one of the witnesses. Dying without issue, he was succeeded by

VI.—Gillies, who does not seem to have served heir to his brother. This Gillies, described as "in Bunachton," and latterly "in Dalmagarry," was a Major in the regiment of Clan Chattan in the '45, and a man of great note and strength. Many authentic anecdotes of his prowess at Culloden are preserved. For instance, when the Campbells pulled down a piece of stone wall forming a protection to the Highlanders, he threw himself into the breach made, and, barricading the passage, killed fourteen men before he fell. Another historian says that Major Gillies Macbean was killed at the first dyke west of the field. By his wife, Miss Macpherson of Lonnie, in Petty, he left at least one son, a minor.

VII. Donald, who on attaining manhood, entered Simon Fraser of Lovat's first regiment, raised in 1757, and was appointed Lieutenant. He was served heir to his uncle Eneas

GILLIES MACBEAN DEFENDING THE DYKE AT CULLODEN.

in 1759, his friends and relations at the time being William Macbean, Attorney-at-Law, London; and Captain Lieutenant Forbes Macbean, both sons of the Rev. Alexander Macbean, of Inverness. The estates, which had been in the hands of creditors for many years, were sold judicially in 1759, and purchased by Simon Fraser of Gibraltar, who acquired at same time the adjoining estate of Borlum.

As the headship of the Macbeans is claimed by severals, I have given as many names as I have met with prior to the time of William 4th. All the male descendants of William 4th of Kinchyle are thought to be extinct, and the headship of the Macbeans must be looked for amongst the descendants of William's collaterals, or of his predecessors.

PART SECOND.—MACBEANS OF DRUMMOND, AND OTHERS IN THE PARISH OF DORES, ETC.

MACBEAN OF DRUMMOND.

IN 1663, Sir Hugh Campbell of Calder feus the lands of Drummond to Alexander Macbean, who, with his wife, Effie Shaw, are infeft in that year. She was a daughter of Angus Shaw, styled of Knocknagail. In 1670, Alexander is dead, and John Macbean—probably Alexander's brother—is found designed Tutor of Drummond. Reference is made same year to a son of the Tutor, but the Christian name is not given. Upon 26th April, 1687, John Macbean enters into a bond for himself and on behalf of his tenants: Evan Macpherson, Donald Gray, John Fraser, weaver, John Bain, Duncan MacConchie, junior, and Finlay MacWilliam, to repay James Dunbar, Merchant in Inverness, such seed as they required of him, in order to lay down their crops, to the extent of fourteen bolls bear. The agreement was, against Martinmas, 1687, to furnish Mr. Dunbar with eighteen bolls of the produce; and, by a marking, it would appear the obligation was implemented in full, prior to February, 1688.

In 1692, John Macbean, above mentioned, as eldest lawful son and heir of Alexander Macbean, is infeft in Drummond. In 1716, John Macbean enters into a contract of marriage with Elspet, third daughter of William Macbean of Kinchyle. This was his second marriage, for Andrew Macbean, lawful son of John Macbean of Drummond, is one of the witnesses to the contract, as is also the notable Gillies Macbean, son of Kinchyle.

There appear to have been questions between the Macbeans of Drummond and their immediate neighbours, the Frasers of Erchite, as to the casting of peats and the cutting of divot. This led to repeated Instruments of Protest and Interruption against the Frasers of Erchite. Although Erchite extended from Loch Ness to Achnabat and Loch Duntelchaig, it had no peat moss, and the disturbances which are recorded as occurring in 1697 and 1711, generally took place at Glaic-na-clach-blea, near Duntelchaig. The marches between Drummond and Erchite had been in dispute of old, but settled by a jury on decree of perambulation, on 31st May, 1669. A deed to which Donald Macbean—who had succeeded John as third of Drummond—is a party, has a goodly number of Macbean signatures. It is written by Ensign William Macbean in Daars, and signed at Drummond, 6th June, 1721, in presence *inter-alios* of William Macbean of Kinchyle, Donald Macbean of Faillie, John Fraser in Dunchea, John

MINOR SEPTS OF CLAN CHATTAN.

Fraser, Tacksman of Duntelchaig, Gillies Macbean, son to Kinchyle, and the said Ensign William Macbean. From the number of Macbean signatures, and particularly that of the famous Major Gillies Macbean, these signatures are photographed, and a *fac-simile* reproduction here given.

FAC-SIMILE OF SIGNATURES TO MACBEAN DEED OF 1721.

Prior to 1751, the Macbeans, who had fallen behind in their estate, parted with Drummond to my great-great-grandfather, Angus Mackintosh, Merchant in Inverness, who is found as owner in that year. Angus Mackintosh was succeeded by his only son, Phineas Mackintosh, Provost of Inverness, who, to his after regret, was tempted by a very high price to sell Drummond to William Fraser of Balnain,

Clerk to the Signet, who acquired step by step all the lands in the Strath of Dores, from Kinchyle to Inverfarigaig, now comprehended under the general name of Aldourie. Provost Phineas Mackintosh, who, as I have said, repented his parting with Drummond, so soon as he was enabled to acquire other lands, bought Drumdevan from the Town of Inverness, and called his new purchase Drummond, in remembrance of his own and his father's original property of Drummond Durris.

Macbeans of Daars, part of Kinchyle.

In 1664, Paul Macbean of Kinchyle wadsets Daars, part of Kinchyle estate, to Donald Macbean in Durris, and Margaret Mackintosh, his spouse, and they are infeft same year.

In 1687, Donald Macbean is dead, as is also his wife, and there being no sons of the marriage, Kinchyle as superior grants an entry to Donald's five daughters—Marjorie, Katherine, Margaret, Mary, and Agnes Macbean—as heiresses-portioners. In 1702, Kinchyle redeems the Wadset, when it is found that all the daughters except Margaret, the second, are married.

The monuments in the churchyard of Dores, if carefully examined, testify strongly to the numbers and influence of the Macbeans within the parish; and there are still several substantial representatives of the clan.

The Macbeans spread in and about Inverness at an early period, and still flourish; one of the tenants on the estate of Mackintosh of Holme, Donald Macbean, is found in 1807, predecessor of the late worthy and honourable Bailie Alexander Macbean of Inverness, father of William Macbean, who presently fills with such credit the position of Provost of Inverness.

Before leaving the Macbeans of Dores and Inverness Parishes, the families of the Rev. Angus Macbean, and of the Rev. Alexander Macbean, both of Inverness, must not be overlooked. The former is generally admitted to have been a younger son of Kinchyle, but neither his propinquity nor that of the Rev. Alexander Macbean has been hitherto absolutely established. From Mr. William Mackay's valuable Inverness and Dingwall Presbytery Records, it is shown that Mr. Angus Macbean is on 17th October, 1683, described as Student in Divinity; and on 19th December, presented to Inverness by Strichen, and, with the approval of Colin, Lord Bishop of Moray, he is inducted, as successor of Mr. Alexander Clerk, to the church of Inverness. By 1687, Mr. Macbean's views had changed, and he absented himself from church meetings, it being recorded that at the meeting on 3rd August, he had been three times absent. The brethren seem to have dealt considerately with him, and appointed a small committee to see and converse with him. The committee reported, 7th September, *inter alia*, that Mr. Macbean asserted that "Presbytery was the only government that God owned in these nations." As also that "Mr. Macbean in his public lectures and sermons did so reflect upon the government of our church, and was like to make such a schism at Inverness as could not be endured by any affected to the present government." At the request of the Magistrates of Inverness, "that all process should be delayed till the next meeting, and that they should use their endeavours to persuade the said Mr. Angus to be more orderly, and to meet with his brethren and satisfy them; which if he would not do, they resolved to leave him to himself if he would not follow their advice;" the matter was adjourned till 5th October, 1687, when it is recorded that Mr. Angus still wilfully absented himself, and neither the Magistrates nor his other friends had in the least prevailed with him. A final effort was made on 19th October. Another deputation was appointed to confer with Mr. Macbean, but by the minutes of meeting of 7th December matters had come to a crisis, it being reported that Mr. Macbean publicly in a service in the Highlands " disowned the Church Government established by law, and publicly demitted his charge of the ministry under the present government, and wilfully deserted his flock; and at same time did publicly exhort and intreat all men whatsoever, to abstain from speaking to him any more in that affair." Mr. Macbean was regularly deposed at Edinburgh, 27th February, 1688, being personally present; and as late as 27th March, 1688, the Presbytery endeavour "to persuade Mr. Angus to return to his duty." The Records of Presbytery are wanting from 19th September, 1688, to 1702, and the latest reference to Mr. Macbean is on 2nd May, 1688, when the sentence of deprivation and deposition of 27th February is ordered to be registered. The after history and early death of Mr. Macbean are well known. It has been stated that he left a son, Mr. Alexander Macbean of Inverness, which may be true, though not absolutely authenticated. Mr. Alexander Macbean, like Mr. Angus, was certainly connected with the Kinchyle family. Mr. Alexander —a good man in many respects, termed the "John Knox" of the North—was an overzealous Hanoverian, for which he got at least a credit from that government not vouchsafed to President Forbes. Mr. Alexander Macbean had been at Fort-William, Douglas, and other places, including Rosemarkie, which received him so ill that he demitted before being finally settled at Inverness. He married one of the daughters of John Macbean, Sheriff Clerk of Inverness. To the marriage contract of the Sheriff Clerk, and his second wife Marjory Baillie, sister of John Baillie of Leys, near Inverness, dated 9th, 15th, and 23rd June, 1732, the Rev. Alexander Macbean is a witness. As the Rev. Alexander Macbean undoubtedly belonged to the church militant, it is not surprising that his descendants, the Forbes-Macbeans, have been and continue hereditary warriors.

PART THIRD.—THE MACBEANS OF FAILLIE.

An influential branch of the Macbeans settled at Faillie, in the parish of Daviot, filling a respectable position for nearly two hundred years.

They probably occupied Faillie a considerable time before they received a heritable right thereto. The first Macbean of Faillie found on record was

1.- -Donald Mac-Gillie-Phadrick, no doubt a cadet of Kinchyle, who, with his wife, Marjorie Macpherson, received a heritable tack of Faillie from James, Earl of Moray, upon 10th February, 1632. Donald is therein described as "in Faillie."

The Stuarts, Earls of Moray, for some time after their acquiring the barony of Strathnairn, and the lordships of Petty and Strathdearn, had been anxious to consolidate their power, and gave heritable rights to many of the occupants, particularly those of Clan Chattan.

The frightful jealousies betwixt the Stuarts and the

FAILLIE HOUSE, DAVIOT, INVERNESS-SHIRE.

Gordons kept the Mackintoshes in constant trouble, whereby their vassals never had any peace. Although extreme measures were taken on more than one occasion by the Earls of Moray against Clan Chattan, the innate vitality and pertinacity of the clan proved successful and victorious.

The following is the description of the lands of Faillie,

extending to a half davoch of land. "All and haill the town and lands of Faillzie, with houses, biggings, yeards, orchards, tofts, crofts, parts, pendicles, and pertinents thereof, used and wont, extending to two ploughs of land, lying within Strathnairn and Sheriffdom of Inverness, as the said lands lye in length and breadth; in houses infield, outfield, muirs, mosses, multures, commonty, pasturage, sheallings, grazings, fishings, free ish and entry, with all and sundry other commoditys and righteous pertinents of the same, used and wont, with the ground right and property of the said lands and others foresaid, and all rights of reversion of the same, and other right title and interest whatsoever thereanent, together with all and sundry contracts, dispositions, charters, infeftments, procuratorys and instruments of resignation, services, retours, precepts and instruments of sasine, tacks and rights of teinds, and all other rights, writs, evidents, titles, and securitys whatsoever of, and concerning the said lands and others foresaid, with all reversions of the same, as well legal as conventionell."

In 1647, mention is made of Donald Macbean, younger of Faillie, and John Macbean, his brother-german. Donald Mac-Gillie-Phadrick was succeeded by his eldest son,

II.—Donald, which became the leading Christian name of the family.

The Macbeans were close allies of their chief, and are to be found at all the Clan and family gatherings; and on 8th October, 1661, Donald Macbean of Faillie is one of the jury at the serving of Lachlan Mackintosh of Torcastle, as heir to his father, William. The inquest was held at Inverness, before Alexander, Earl of Moray, Sheriff Principal, personally presiding.

Donald Macbean, the II., was succeeded by his son,

III.—Donald. Donald's wife was Anna, eldest daughter of William Macbean of Kinchyle. Mrs. Anna Macbean is infeft in a jointure furth of Achlaschoile and Mid-town of Faillie; Mr. John Macbean, schoolmaster at Daviot, acting as her attorney.

Donald procures a charter of confirmation from Charles, Earl of Moray, as heir to his grandfather, Donald I., on 15th July, 1707.

Donald Macbean having died without male issue, was succeeded by his brother,

IV.—William, who is found in the years 1741 to 1758, and in 1749, on 15th January, receives a confirmation of his tack from the Earl of Moray.

This William Macbean's father, Donald the III., unfortunately became security for people of his own name, particularly John Macbean, writer in Inverness, whereby his successors were impoverished, and the estate, long in the hands of creditors, brought to a compulsory sale. The nature of the fatal involvement was this:

John, Earl of Cromarty, was very impecunious, and his estates sequestered, and placed locally by the court in charge of John Macbean, writer in Inverness, named above. Mr. Macbean, according to rule, had to find caution for his intromissions, and in 1724, Lachlan Mackintosh of Mackintosh, George Cuthbert of Castlehill, and Donald Macbean of Faillie, became cautioners.

This Factory was not a success—Mr. Macbean's representative and cautioners being called to account for enormous sums. It was alleged for the deceased and his cautioners that the messengers and officers of the law employed by him, were deforced and otherwise hindered by "Bangstrie," and oppression from uplifting the rents of the Cromartie estate, and that they were only responsible for Mr. Macbean's actual intromissions. The arbiters so far gave effect to the defences, and in 1744 limited the decree to a sum of £3,211 4s. 6d. Scots,—a considerable sum in those days—to which had to be added great costs.

Castlehill estate fell under control of the court as insolvent, and Mr. Macbean's own estate was insignificant after payment of debts.

The whole debt, with interests and costs, fell upon Mackintosh and Faillie, and though Mackintosh had to pay in full in the first instance, time was given to Faillie by his chief. The burden, however, was too heavy, and the estate was of little use to the Macbeans after 1744.

In 1756 William Macbean consents to Mackintosh's reclaiming the Laggan lands, signing the deed of consent as brother-german and representative of the deceased Donald Macbean of Faillie. The deed is also signed by many others of Clan Chattan, including Alexander Macphail of Inverernie, eldest son and heir, served and retoured to the deceased, Robert Macphail of Inverernie; by Robert Mackintosh, Tacksman of Termite, eldest son in life of the deceased Lachlan Mackintosh of Strone; by William Mackintosh of Aberarder, heir and representative of the deceased William Mackintosh of Aberarder, his grandfather; by William Mackintosh of Holme, eldest son and heir of the deceased John Mackintosh of Holme; and by John Mackintosh of Culclachie, eldest son and heir of the deceased Angus Mackintosh of Culclachie. All these heads of Clan Chattan sign at Gask, in Strathnairn, upon the 27th October, 1756, in presence of Donald Macbean, son of Donald

FAILLIE BRIDGE, DAVIOT, INVERNESS-SHIRE.

Macbean, vintner in Inverness; and Alexander Fraser, farmer in the Mains of Tordarroch.

This document is peculiarly interesting in respect that it is dated several years after the abolition of the Heritable Jurisdiction Acts, and clan associations.

William Macbean was succeeded by his son,

V.—Donald, who in 1768 is retoured heir to his father.

He appears to have served in France, holding the rank of Captain, and to have been so long absent from Scotland that when he attempted to remove one or two people in the year 1770, prior to the sale of the estate, which had then become inevitable, defences were given in alleging that he was an alien, and a professed Papist, incapable of holding landed property. Captain Macbean was very indignant, and his holograph observations upon the defences show that his long absence abroad did not by any means do away with his great natural shrewdness, and appreciation of business matters.

It is to be feared that Captain Macbean's long services abroad did not benefit him much pecuniarly. In 1768 he appears to have interested himself in his estates for the first time, and intrusted his affairs to the care of Mr. James Fraser of Gortuleg.

By 1770 the affairs had come to a crisis, when a sale was made to MacGillivray of Dunmaglass. Whether Captain Macbean was married or left male issue, I am not aware—the last occupant of the name of Macbean being Mrs. Ketty Macbean. I have many of her letters, running on from 1750 to 1780, and I presume she was Captain Macbean's step-mother, for she never refers to him. She removed from Faillie at the sale, and her letters are afterwards dated from Dundee. From these I should infer that she was an excellent specimen of the kindly and true hearted-Highland lady of the past. The house of Faillie, with a few ancient trees, stands imposingly on a high bank of the river Nairn, the sketch on page 43, taken expressly for this work, giving a very good

MINOR SEPTS OF CLAN CHATTAN.   49

idea of the place. The bridge, which is also given, is well done, and is the first erected by General Wade on his new road from Inverness to the south. Across this bridge Prince Charles rode after the battle on his flight from Culloden towards the west; and a very fine picture showing his passage over the Faillie bridge was exhibited in London some years ago, drawing much attention from every Highlander who saw it. During the many years Faillie was occupied by the present Sheriff Fraser of Portree as agricultural tenant, the place was known all over the north for its breed of Highland cattle.

PART FOUR.—THE MACBEANS OF TOMATIN, ETC.

The pretty estate of Tomatin, in the parish of Moy and Lordship of Strathdearn, is, and for more than two hundred and fifty years has been, in possession of this family. More fortunate than the Macbeans of Kinchyle, Drummond, and Faillie, they have not only preserved their original estate, but added within the last half-century the estate of Free, lying adjacent. Strathdearn, since the opening of the Highland railway by Forres, has been much isolated. It is, however, destined to renewed life and activity, for the new and direct line to Perth, *via* Aviemore, intersects the district. A sketch of the viaduct across the
G

river Findhorn, the greatest in the North, is here given. The structure, still in progress, on its north side rests upon Tomatin estate.

THE FINDHORN VIADUCT AT TOMATIN.

The first Macbean to acquire the property was I.—Bean Macbean, styled Bean-Mac-Coil-vic-Gillie Phadrick, " in Moril-more."

The original charter, by James, Earl of Moray, is dated 16th December, 1639, and runs in favour of the said Bean, his heirs male and assignees. The similarity of the names would indicate a close connection with the family of Faillie; and I am inclined to think that Bean, first of Tomatin, was younger son of Donald Mac-Gillie-Phadrick, first of Faillie, referred to in the previous chapter.

Bean, first Tomatin, was succeeded by his son
II.—Eugenius, otherwise Evan, who was infeft in 1677, as heir to his father, Bean, in the lands, on precept from Alexander, Earl of Moray, dated 18th February, 1677. This Evan consequently fell into difficulties, and the estate was adjudicated by William Macbean, apparently his brother, Burgess of Inverness; who, on the death of Evan without male issue, entered into possession of Tomatin under the adjudication, and destined the estate to his son, Bean, whose son,

III.—John Macbean, married Janet Mackintosh, daughter of Mackintosh of Dalmagerry. Their contract of marriage is dated at Inverness and Tomatin on 11th and 24th April, 1688. The description of lands in the contract is as follows:—
"All and haill the plough town and lands of Tomatin, with houses, biggings, yards, barns, byres, mosses, muirs, sheilings, grazings, outsetts, annexis, connexis, parts, pendicles, and remanent universal pertinents, pertaining and belonging thereto, lying within the Lordship of Strathdearn, Parochin of Moy, and Sheriffdom of Inverness." As it has a goodly number of Macbean witnesses I give their names and designations, viz:—Gillies Macbean of Wester Draikies; Donald Macbean,

Merchant, Burgess of Inverness; Angus Macbean, younger, Writer in Inverness; Mr. Alexander Cumming, Minister of Moy; and Alexander Mackintosh of Holme.

This John was a prudent and careful man, and kept his papers in good order. There is a Bible dated 1640, which is much treasured by the family on account of the number of births, deaths, and marriages, engrossed from an early date on its blank pages. John is found in the years 1682 to 1730.

In 1740, designated younger of Tomatin —

IV.—William Macbean is found. William married Jean, daughter of Lachlan Macpherson of Strathnoon. In Mr. Macbean's latter will and testament, dated Tomatin, 2nd July, 1742, he appoints Strathnoon to be his executor, and to account to Ludovic Macbean, his only child in life, for his intromissions. He further appoints Gillies Macbean, tacksman of Dalmagerry, and Donald and John Macbean, his brothers german, to call, if necessary, the executor to account, in the interests of his son.

Ludovic must have been in pupillarity at this time, for the above Gillies, Donald, and John are appointed his tutors, until he arrive at the age when he can choose curators. Mr. William Macbean's will was written by Mr. Donald Macqueen, younger of Corrybrough, and signed in his presence and that of Lachlan Mackintosh, 2nd of Raigmore. Ludovic's predecessors, William and John, do not appear to have taken out a title to the estate, for Ludovic is entered by James, Earl of Moray, as heir to his grand-uncle, Evan. William Macbean had two brothers, John and Donald, who discharge their portions in his favour, dated at Dalmagerry, 18th February,

1742, written by Gillies Macbean, son of Kinchyle, and witnessed by the writer, by Bean Macbean, residenter at Dalmagerry, Donald Macbean, student there, and David Macbean, schoolmaster at Dalmagerry. In 1760 the above

TOMATIN HOUSE, INVERNESS-SHIRE.

V.—Ludovic appears in possession, and was one of the most important of his race, having established a mercantile connection with Glasgow, not only enabling him to place his family on a high footing, but also to benefit in no small degree struggling Northerners, who through his influence obtained excellent positions at home, and in the West Indies and the Plantations.

Mr. Macbean married Ann Smith, and had a family of ten, of whom I need only refer to William, the sixth, and Duncan, the seventh sons.

For nearly fifty years the Tomatin Macbeans may be said to have been at the head of Highlanders and all Highland movements in Glasgow. In his factor's accounts there are several charges for supplying 'tartan for Ludovic' when a child. He died, greatly lamented, and was succeeded by his son, VI.—William Macbean, 6th of his family, as before mentioned. This William did not long survive, dying unmarried at Tomatin on the 9th June, 1822. Mr. Macbean lived a good deal in the North, and seems to have farmed the lands of Balphadrick, near Inverness. He was succeeded by his brother, VII.—Duncan Macbean. This Duncan was extensively engaged in business in Glasgow, and was also connected with the West Indies, having also a house of business in London, and maintained, indeed surpassed, the useful position occupied by his father. Duncan married Jean Moore, 7th November, 1814, and had a family of thirteen. One of his daughters, with her family, live in the North-West of Canada, and proving their affection for the old country and kin, have called their place "Glen Chattan."

In this Mr. Macbean's time, Celtic feeling, which has now arrived at such a great pitch, began to assert itself in Glasgow, and Mr. Macbean was at its head. I have been so much struck with the stalwartness of Glasgow Celts at the 15th anniversary of a festive gathering held on the 17th

March, 1851, with Mr. Macbean as croupier, that I cannot resist making one or two quotations from the toast list, The number of toasts was actually 28. No. 14—"Tìr nam beann, nan gleann, 's nan breacan." No. 18—"Cridhe eutrom, agus sporan trom." No. 28—"Am fear nach treig a chompanach." It may be doubted whether such a list in these degenerate days, if gone through as systematically as was wont to be done, would not have the effect of placing every one under the table. I select the above three, and draw attention to the change that has taken place in the first, and should be glad to know when the alteration to the present form first occurred. The Caledonian Bank was founded in 1838, and the words on it, "Nan Gaisgeach," instead of "Nam breacan," are now universally used. Duncan was succeeded by his eldest son and third child,

VIII.—Ludovic Macbean, who succeeded his father on 11th May, 1854, and died unmarried, 10th January, 1862, being succeeded by his brother,

IX.—William Macbean, 11th of his father's family, who became a colonel in the army, and married Miss Janetta Macbean of the Leghorn Macbeans, (she is presently married to Colonel Eden), died without issue, 3rd August, 1879, when he was succeeded by his brother the present

X.—Lachlan Macbean, 12th of his family, born 16th February, 1833. Mr. Macbean married on the 10th June, 1862, Miss Jane Macbean Moore, and he, like his father, had thirteen children. Duncan Moore, his second son, now in Natal, born 19th March, 1864, is his heir, and will ultimately succeed to, and represent the old and respected family of Tomatin.

Many eminent Macbeans have spread over the North and abroad. Take Sir James Macbean, a native of Inverness; the Macbeans of Ardclach, of whom sprung the late worthy and learned Mr. Eneas Macbean, W.S., friend and intimate of Sir Walter Scott; the Macbeans, long Consuls at Leghorn, afterwards at Rome, at whose hospitable board were for years to be found the élite of Northern Scottish gentry, gatherings which after the lapse of thirty years I gladly recall; and last, but not least, the late Major-General William Macbean, V.C., a most gallant and distinguished officer, a man of whom Inverness, his birth place, and all Macbeans, may well be proud. A bust of General Macbean, gifted by his relatives, has just been placed, with all honour, in the Town Hall of Inverness.

No. III.—THE MACPHAILS OF INVERAIRNIE.

In Sir Eneas Mackintosh's Memoirs of Clan Chattan the Macphails appear in the list as No. 14 of the tribes, and that they took protection of Mackintosh about 1500.

In the Kinrara History of the Mackintoshes, it is said that in the time of Duncan the 8th (1456-1496) lived "Paul Gow, good sir of Sir Andrew Macphail, the priest, of whom the Clan Phail had their beginning."

This Sir Andrew, grandson of Paul, first of the Macphails, according to the Kinrara history, wrote the third of the three histories of Clan Chattan, upon which Kinrara founds in part his history. He adds that Sir Andrew's history began with Shaw, the 1st Mackintosh, and ended with William 15th, murdered at Strathbogie in 1550.

The Rev. Lachlan Shaw, the historian, when dealing with the parishes of Daviot and Dunlichty, refers to "Macphail of Inverairnie, the Chief of that ancient tribe of Clan Chattan."

The family did not acquire Inverairnie until 1631, but the name is to be found at a much earlier period, and was common among ecclesiastics. The first Macphail I have noticed was named Gillies. He died prior to 1500, his place of residence not being mentioned. He married Margaret Mackintosh, who bore to him John, Paul, Alison, Margaret,

Catherine, and Agnes. In 1496 David Dunbar of Durris pursues Mackintosh and the following, his men and dependents—"Gillies Macphail, Donald MacGillivray, Farquhar Eachin's son, Auchan MacRuari, and Alexander MacAllister," for the wrongous occupation and labouring of the lands of Durris, with the pertinents lying within the Sheriffdom of Inverness, "for the space of one year last bye past."

In 1558 Donald MacDonald vic Phail is found, and in the same year John Reoch MacPhail.

In 1560 Sir John MacPhail is one of the Procurators in the Sheriff Court of Inverness.

In 1561 James MacWilliam vic Phail is found.

After the Reformation the Macphails appear in force as ecclesiastics. We find Mr. Andrew Macphail, reader at Petty and Bracklie in 1574; settled at Kirkhill 1575; translated to Kingussie in 1581, and to Dores in 1590.

In a deed dated at Inverness, 26th April, 1594, two of of the witnesses are "Andrew Macphail, Minister of the word of God at Croy, and Severinus Macphail, Minister of the Church of Petty." Neither of these gentlemen's names appear in the *Fasti* as holding office in Croy and Petty.

There is notice of Souverane Makpharlane or Macphail as having been presented by James VI. to Alvie in 1585-6, and that he was continued to 1594, no doubt the same person above referred to as Minister of Petty.

Several Macphails are found in the County of Sutherland in the early part of the 17th Century, and were burgesses of Dornoch.

The Macphails did not acquire a heritable right to Inverairnie until the year 1631, when Hugh Rose, then of Kilravock, in respect of a thousand pounds scots granted a wadset right and long tack of Inverairnie to

I.—Duncan Macphail, therein described as "of Inverairnie." This original grant is dated 19th May, 1631. The lands of Inverairnie, facing the River Nairn, lie within the Barony of Strathnairn and Parish of Dalarossie, and have for more than a century been divided, the upper portion next to Farr having been acquired by the family of Farr, and still forming part of that estate, the other and lower portion adjoining Wester Lairgs, being acquired by Macgillivray of Dunmaglass. Both portions are watered by the River Airnie, which falls into the Nairn adjoining to Lower Inverairnie; and forming a portion thereof, lies on the high grounds betwixt Strathnairn and Strathdearn, a very extensive muir called the "Shalvanach," of old capital grazing, and now excellent shooting grounds.

The Inverairnie estate also comprehended the lands of Duglass, and Duletter, in Strathdearn, practically adjoining, but facing the River Findhorn and the south. These lands formed that part of the present estate of Glenmazeran acquired from the Mackintoshes of Aberarder, successors to Inverairnie in Strathdearn.

The next Macphail I find is

II.—Paul Macphail in 1689, probably a grandson of the above Duncan. Paul Macphail acquired on 13th March, 1689, from Kilravock, the reversionary rights to the lands, in respect of a feu duty of two hundred and nine merks and other prestations. Paul is infeft on 7th December, 1689. He married, first—Elspet Shaw of Tordarroch, and by her had two sons, Duncan and Robert. Paul married, secondly—a lady described as "Jean Forbes, niece to the laird of Culloden." Wishing to favour a son by the second marriage, Paul Macphail made a new arrangement with Kilravock on 4th July, 1699. By Jean Forbes, Paul Macphail had a son, John, described in 1765 as "now Surveyor of the Customs at Fort-William," who took infeftment as heir of provision in 1754. To fortify the title of the son by the second marriage, Paul Macphail assigned his estate to William Macphail, merchant in Inverness, and Margaret Mackintosh, his spouse.

But William Macphail favoured the heir male, and on 15th September, 1716, gave over his rights to Robert, eldest surviving son of Paul Macphail. Paul was succeeded by his second, but eldest surviving son,

III.—Robert Macphail, and in 1721 Robert is in full possession of the estate. He died in 1743, when he was succeeded by his son,

IV.—Alexander Macphail, who made up titles to the estate in 1756. In 1759-1760 Alexander, the heir male, at great cost settled with John Macphail before mentioned, the heir of provision.

Alexander Macphail was now undisputed owner of Inverairnie, but the consideration paid to his relative, John, and the litigation with Kilravock, the Superior, proved fatal, and necessitated a sale of the estate.

Thus the weakness of Paul, second in this list, and the cupidity of his second wife, brought about the ruin of the

family. Kilravock by himself, and others in right of the
large feu, attempted to take possession of the estate and
remove Alexander. He fought hard for years to maintain
his position, having at length to succumb, when Inverairnie
was acquired by Farr and Dunmaglass jointly, the estate being
divided.

It was with Dunmaglass Inverairnie chiefly dealt, and numerous transactions passed in form of money and documents, before a final clearance.

Alexander Macphail, as formerly mentioned, signed the Bond in favour of Mackintosh redeeming the Laggan lands in 1756, as head of the Macphails. In his struggles to retain his estate Alexander executed a transfer to a relative, Paul Macphail. The deed is written by Alexander himself, and was signed at Inverairnie on the 14th April, 1763, in presence of John Macphail, youngest lawful son of the late Robert Macphail of Inverairnie, Donald Macphail, tenant in old town of Inverairnie, and Donald Macphail, in Lynrich of Farr. I shall only make one further reference to Alexander Macphail, whose ill-fortune I deplore. Before finally settling with William MacGillivray of Dunmaglass, documents, as I said, were given, one obligation coming into the hands of the notorious Farquhar MacGillivray of Dalcrombie as doer for Dunmaglass. I will mention it in poor Inverairnie's own words, from a petition to the Sheriff craving release from prison. Inverairnie says "that notwithstanding his having settled with Dunmaglass, Farquhar MacGillivray of Dalcrombie, without having any special mandate from the said Captain William MacGillivray, who is out of the kingdom, in Georgia, upon Monday last, the 6th current (December, 1773), came with a party of 12 men, armed with guns and staves, and upon the high road attacked the petitioner, and by the strong hand held him about two hours in the snow, by force and violence, without having a caption or any warrand, or messenger or officer of the law with him," and had him conveyed to prison.

Sheriff Macqueen on the 9th December, on a petition by Inverairnie, ordered answers within forty-eight hours. By a marking on the paper dated 13th December, no answers had been given in. There were towards the end of last century no two more determined and unscrupulous men in the County of Inverness than John Macpherson in Ballachroan, and Farquhar MacGillivray of Dalcrombie.

Not only have the Macphails disappeared from Inverairnie, but there are none of the name occupying land in Strathnairn and Strathdearn. The last I knew was Mr. Angus Macphail, tenant in Mid Lairgs under Mackintosh, a most worthy man, who with his excellent helpmate, had a high and deserved reputation in the churches. Some of his descendants, I believe, are in Melbourne, Victoria. Whether there be an heir male of Inverairnie I know not, but should anyone—for instance the rising counsel of the name—think he has a claim, now is the time to establish his right to the honour.

There are several of this Sept who now sign "M'Fall," pronounced phonetically, being the genetive of Paul, a form of Phàil, Phòil, or Pòl, many Gaelic names standing in phonetic form, amongst whom may be mentioned Captain Crawford M'Fall, of the King's Own Light Infantry.

MACQUEEN.

NO. IV.—THE MACQUEENS.

ALTHOUGH originally only an offshoot of the Hebridean Macqueens, who owed allegiance to the Lord of the Isles; the Macqueens of Corrybrough, who settled in Strathdearn, and in time sent out cadets who occupied much of the valley of the Findhorn in the centre of Inverness and Nairn, may be said to have occupied the position of head of the haill name. The Rev. Lachlan Shaw referring to Corrybrough, describes it as "the property of Donald Macqueen, Chief of that branch of Clan Chattan."

The Macqueens were known as Clan Revan, and stand in Sir Eneas Mackintosh's list as No. 10. The circumstances under which the Macqueens left the west coast and settled in Strathdearn are:—"Early in the 15th century Malcolm Beg Mackintosh, 10th Mackintosh, married Mora Macdonald of Muidart, and with the bride came, as was the custom, several of her kinsmen, who took up their abode near her new home. Amongst others were Revan-Mac-Mulmor Mac-Angus, of whom the Clan Revan are descended, and Donald Mac-Gillandrish, of whom the Clan Andrish."

In an old MS. the above Revan is noted as Roderick Dhu Revan Macqueen, and that he fought under Mackintosh at the Battle of Harlaw, 1411. From this date my line is broken to 1594, when Donald Macqueen is found as heritor of Corrybrough. A William Macqueen, styled "of Corrybrough," is noted in 1593; and in 1543 Allister Macqueen and William Macqueen are described as of Clan Chattan. At the Reformation the name of Macqueen is prominent among

CORRYBROUGH HOUSE.

ecclesiastics, and I will particularly refer to William Macqueen, Parson at Assynt, afterwards Sub-Dean of Ross. In the *Fasti*, under Assynt, he is not recorded. In January, 1577, he is presented to Tain, and is described "as probably a convert from the Romish faith," and in 1578 is presented to the

Sub-Deanery of Ross, and under date 1583 there is a reference to the alienation of his manse at the Chanonry of Ross. His character did not stand high, and the following account of his deposition is interesting as shewing ecclesiastical procedure against delinquent clergymen, at an early period after the Reformation, prior by many years in date to any existing ecclesiastical record for Ross.

"The extract of the process led and deducit contrar William M'Kquyne, pretendit Sub-dene of Ros, befoir the Synodall Assemblie of the Ministerie of Ros, holden at the Channorie thereof, secundo Octobris sessione secunda ejusdem synodi anno dominy 1594.

"The quhilk day ane citation being producit be the moderator and brethren of the presbyterie of Tayne dewlie execute and indorsate whereby the said William was peremtorily summonit to the said secund day of the said synod and year of God forsaid. The tenour of the quhilk summondis and execution thairof followis.

"The brethren of the presbyterie of Tayne to our lovites John Ros executoris heirof, we charge you that this citation sene ye pas and lawfullie summond, warne and chairge William M'Quhyne, pretendit Sub-dene of Ros, to compeir before the bretheryne of the Synodall Assemblie of Ros within the Channorie thairof the secund day of October nixt to cum beand the secund day of the Synodall, to bring and produce with him the pretendit gift collationn and admissionn of the said Sub-denerie giff if he ony hes, and to heir and sie the samyn cassit rescindit and declairit null, and to heff bene of na strenthe foirce nor effect, fra the beginning, now, and in all tyme cuming, for dyvers cawsis and reasonis. They are to say, pluralitie of benefices, adulterie, with dyveris wtheris, and that conforme to ane act and ordinance maid under his owin subscriptionn at the tyme of his said pretended admission, with certification to him that whether he compeir or nocht at the time and place forsaid, the said Synodall Assemblie will proceid and minister justice in the said matter according to all equity and guid conscience. The quhilk to do we committ to you, etc., etc. Be this our precept, delivering the same be

I

you dewlie execute and indorsate again to the berar, at Tayne the tent day of September 1594 yeiris.

"The tennour of the execution follows:— Upon the 23rd day of September the yeir of God 1594 yeiris, I John Ross executor hereof within written, past at the command hereof and lawfully summoned warnit and chargit William M'Kquyne, pretendit Sub dene of Ros, within written, being in Alexander Spence, his house within the Channonrie of Ros for the tyme, and delyverit ane copie heirof to his wyfe, he being sleeping in the meantyme, in his bed within the same house, to compeir before the brethren of the Synodal Assemblie of Ros, day, yeir and place within written, to the effect and for the causes within specefeit, with certificationn likeweys within mentionate. And this I did before these witnesses, Alexander Spence, indweller in the Channonrie of Ros, and William Watsone, with others diverse, and for the mair verification hereof to this my indorsation, my signet and subscription manuall are affixit (Sic Subscribitúr cum Signo) Johne Ros with my hand executor heirof.

"That day the summondis producit being callit, compeirit Alexander Ruthven as procurator for the said William, and granted him to have been summonit to that day and receivit ane copie of the summondis, and objectit allanerlie against the execution of the said summondis, allegeand the same was not relevant in respect the same was not raisit upon the premonition of fourtie days according to the Act of Parliament, as he allegit. Notwithstanding of the quhilk reason proponit by the said Alexander Ruthven, procurator foresaid, the kirk found the said execution to be lawfull, notwithstanding of the foresaid allegiance, because there is no such form accustomed or even practised in the kirk in proceedings against members, office-bearers in the same, but that they may lawfully proceed against any such member within their own jurisdiction upon such time and premonition as best pleases them. And further it is notoriously known to the haill brethren of the Synodall that the said William who was summoned, was dwelling with his haill family in his own town of Arkindithe, the haill time of the holding of the Synodall, which place of Arkindithe lies within one mile of the Channonrie foresaid, where the said Synodall was holden for a time, and so might have compeared presently at all times before the said Synodall, and he willfully and disobediently absented himself. In respect of the which, the said allegiance proponit by Alexander

Ruthven as procurator foresaid, was repelled by the brethren of the Synodall Assemblie, and found that they might proceed with the principal cause for the reasons after following, Primo, plurality of benefices, as the Parsonage and Vicarage of Assynt, and sub-deanery of Ross. Secundo, adulterie with Elizabeth Ross, he being married with Margaret Gourlay in Kennoway in Fife. Tertio, by virtue of an act of the kirk, subscribed by himself, made at the Channonrie of Ross the time of his pretended admission bearing by a special clause contained thereuntil, that afterwards if at any time he were found guilty of any of these heads of accusations as were laid to his charge, the time of his said pretended admission should be null and of no avail as though the same had never been granted, which points and accusations being thoroughly reasoned, tried and examined by the moderator and haill brethren of the Synodall, and namely having considered his whole course of life, being profane and dissolute from the beginning and to have (blank in the MS.) himself in the kirk, by obtaining of compulsitors of hearing against the Bishop for the time, for advocating of him to the benefice of the said Sub-deanerie, the haill brethren of the said Synodall finds him guilty and culpable in the foresaid crimes, as also having considered his dissolute and slanderous life ever since the time of his said pretended admission; therefore, in respect of the premises, the haill brethren of the Synodall with one consent, rescinds, casses, and annuls the pretended admission, and decerns the same to have been null from the beginning and in all time coming, conform to the tenor of the said summons and the act foresaid under his own subscription. Extracted furth of the books of the Synodall Assembly of Ross, subscribed by the clerk thereof."

Thus the brethren, without calling witnesses or putting any one on oath, determined and pronounced extreme judgment. The poor sub-dean was expelled, but his two benefices were worth looking after.

I have a Bond holograph of the Sub-dean, dated 25th May, 1592, acknowledging a loan of 100 merks, in which the following singular error occurs. The period of repayment is the "fifth day of August next to come, called our Lady day."

In the early part of the seventeenth century the Macqueens came well to the front. Three landholders, Donald Macqueen of Corrybrough; John Macqueen of Little Corrybrough; and Sweyn Macqueen of Raigbeg, are parties to the Bond of Union among the Clan Chattan, signed at Termit of Petty on the 4th of April, 1609, one of the witnesses to the Bond being Mr. Donald Macqueen, Parson of Petty. This person was in good circumstances, lending 2,000 merks to the Earl of Moray, receiving therefor in wadset the two plough lands of Midcoul, in the parish of Bracklie, by deed signed at Castle Stuart, 18th July, 1628. To his Letter of Reversion of same date, Mr. Donald Macqueen adhibits his signature thus, "Donald M'Queen, Persone of Pettie," and affixes his "Seal of Arms." The reverend gentleman married first, Isobel Mackintosh, and secondly Agnes Douglas. With Donald Macqueen of Corrybrough, found in 1594, we arrive on firm ground, but some early Macqueens may be noted. On 21st March, 1559-60, there is note of a legal contention betwixt John Macqueen and John vic Alexander, anent the theft of a black horse. In the same year Donald Mac Iain Dhu Macqueen is noted, also William Macqueen, indweller in Inverness. In 1561-62 William Macqueen is a leading Procurator in the Sheriff Court of Inverness; also acts as a Notary Public. Under date 29th March, 1561, William vic Iain Dhu Macqueen, probably the same person, acts as Procurator for the Parishioners of Kilmuir and Suddie in certain legal proceedings.

In 1562 William Macqueen and others are summoned by

Mungo Monipennie, Dean of Ross, for the spulzie of victual ont of the lands of Ardersier. On 17th April, 1562, Alexander Macqueen finds Finlay Macqueen Mackintosh as his cautioner, to keep the peace with John Ogilvie in Urlarust of Petty. John Mac Iain Macqueen finds caution to stand trial for an alleged theft of cattle, and on 7th July, 1562, Donald Macqueen and Iver Macqueen are noted.

During the 17th century it is mentioned that there were twelve heritors of the name in the shires of Inverness and Nairn. Amongst others may be mentioned in Nairnshire, Donald Macqueen of Reatt; Macqueen of Carnoch and Drynachan; Alexander Macqueen of Daless; and Sweyn vic Lachlan Macqueen in Little Quilichan of the Streens. In Inverness-shire the principal cadets were Macqueen of Pollochaig, Macqueen of Little Raig, Macqueen of Clune, &c., &c.

I.—Donald Macqueen, whom I place as first of Corrybrough, is found in 1594, 1609, 1615, and 1623. His son George is mentioned in 1620, who, if married, died without issue. Donald's brother John, with his wife Catherine Fraser, are noted under date 5th June, 1620. Donald dies in or prior to 1623, for in that year his nephew

II.—Angus succeeded, whose mother's name was Agnes Mackintosh, and his wife's name Isobel Farquharson. Angus is noted in 1632, and in 1649 grants a wadset right over Glenkirk. He is one of the signatories to "the Bond by the name of Clan Chattan to their chief, Mackintosh," dated Kincairne, 19th November, 1664. Angus was succeeded by his son

III.—Donald, who died in 1676, having married Mary Cuthbert of Castlehill. Their son, also

IV.—Donald, is noted in 1685 and 1697 as a Commissioner of Supply for the County of Inverness. He married Jean Dallas of Cantray, and was succeeded by his son

V.—James, who married, 29th September, 1711, Katherine Fraser of Culduthel. One of his daughters, Anna, is contracted in marriage in 1733 with Robert Mackintosh, son of Mackintosh of Stron. James, then younger of Corrybrough, was captain in the Clan Chattan regiment in the rising of 1715, and was fortunate enough to escape the consequences. The closest friendship existed between James Macqueen and his son, Sheriff Macqueen, with the Mackintoshes, and James, at Glenkirk, 29th October, 1756, signs the consent to Mackintosh reclaiming the Loch Laggan lands, as eldest son and representative of Donald Macqueen of Corrybrough. He died in 1762. His daughter, Elizabeth, married Lachlan Mackintosh, second of Raigmore. James Macqueen was succeeded by his son

VI.—Donald Macqueen, the well-known Sheriff-Substitute of Inverness, an authority in Celtic literature, long the valued neighbour and confidential adviser of the Mackintoshes. As early as 1740-41, I observe that he transacts business for the family, he being then a law student in Edinburgh. He married in 1742, Margaret Shaw of Dell, and lived to a great age, not dying till 1792. A discreditable affair connected with the Sheriff, then in venerable old age, and an invalid daughter, occurred in 1792, in which John Grant, Sheriff Clerk Depute of Inverness, was a prominent actor.

In the Circuit Court held at Inverness, 2nd May, 1793, the foresaid John Grant was found guilty of forgery, and after the case was remitted to the High Court of Justiciary, sentenced to transportation for life. Sheriff Macqueen, erroneously described in Burke as dying in 1789, was succeeded by his son VII.—Captain Donald Macqueen, a man of undoubted ability, but over hasty, in whose time the affairs of the family, formerly involved, became critical. An intention of re-establishment occurred in 1758, when John Macqueen, of Potosi in Jamaica, by will ordered the estate of Muirtown in the County of Moray, to be purchased and settled on the family of the testator's cousin, Donald Macqueen of Corrybrough. But at John's death, his estate was found to be inconsiderable. There are few Macqueens

FAC-SIMILE OF RECEIPT BY DONALD FRASER TO THE CHIEF OF MACKINTOSH, 1744.

at present in the parish of Moy, and none on the estate of Corrybrough, which was unhappily cleared by a notorious speculating surveyor named Smith. The estate, originally two ploughs of land, had been enlarged by the acquisition of the plough of Raigbeg, and the plough of Morclune, raising the whole estate to a davoch of land extending to seven thousand acres. Naturally, Corrybrough did not remain long with the speculator, and was acquired about 1844 for £12,000, by an Englishman named Malkin. The new family did not re-people

72   MINOR SEPTS OF CLAN CHATTAN.

the estate, but it is only just to say that they bear a kindly reputation, and have shown attention to the family of Donald Fraser after-mentioned. Contrast Corrybrough of to-day, without

ANVIL OF DONALD FRASER, "CAPTAIN OF THE FIVE."

a single tenant of land, with the positions under the Macqueens in 1811. In Lyn Evan there were Donald Mackintosh and Alexander Mackintosh. In old Town, Donald Macqueen. In half of Ballimore and Miln Croft, Alexander Mackintosh and Alexander Macdonald. In the other half, Alexander Macdonald and Alexander Macqueen. In Dalnaban, James Macqueen. In Tombreck, James Macqueen and Donald MacGillivray. In Glenkirk, James Macqueen and Angus Macqueen. In upper Corrybrough beg, Alexander Macbean and Alexander Macqueen, In lower Corrybrough beg, Donald Macqueen and widow Macqueen. In Battanmore, widow Elspet Macdonald. In Dalreoch, William Chisholm and Donald Diamond. The total rental in 1811 was £314 1s. 10d., furth of 13 possessions, on which, perhaps 100 souls were nourished, and there is a note on the back of the rent roll that there were no arrears. The dispossessed people emigrated chiefly to the United States, and in the year 1890 their settlement in Ohio was visited by one of the respected Macdougall family, who reported "that they had formed a prosperous colony in the State of Ohio, and he found that many of them spoke the Gaelic well." Writing in 1827, Mr. Campbell Mackintosh, Town Clerk of Inverness, refers to Morclune "as the place where the present mansion house of Corrybrough is built."

Captain Donald Macqueen received a commission at a very early age in the regiment raised by Lord Macdonald, and in his Lordship's letter to old Corrybrough, dated 26th January, 1778, he expresses himself thus, that "it did him great honour to have the sons of chieftains in the regiment, and as the Macqueens have been invariably attached to our family, to whom I believe we owe our existence, I am proud of the nomination."

This very gratifying tribute shews clearly the origin of

K

the Macqueens, and that though the Macqueens of Corrybrough had for centuries allied themselves with, and become incorporated in Clan Chattan, and still are of it, there are numerous Macqueens in the Hebrides, who were and continued to be dependent on the Macdonalds. I note in passing that one of the name, Macqueen of Braxfield, has been selected for vilification by a deceased hysteric-spasmodic performer, not his first offence, having regard neither to truth, nor the feelings of Braxfield's living descendants.

Captain Macqueen married on 27th April, 1792, Elizabeth, daughter of Hugh Fraser of Brightmony, great-grandson of Malcolm Fraser of Culduthel. He served in the American war, and I possess one of his letters from New York in 1780. He died in 1813, and his widow in 1827. Their family consisted of nine, Donald; Hugh, the well-known Writer to the Signet, died in 1836; James, died young; Dr. Alexander, 3rd Foot, died 1845; William, Captain 25th Madras Infantry, died 1829; Captain Simon, died 1837; Eneas, Lieutenant 49th Madras Infantry, died 1837; John Fraser, Q.C., died 1881; and Lachlan, Lieutenant-Colonel 3rd Madras Cavalry, both of whom hereafter.

VIII.—Donald Macqueen, Captain 2nd Madras Cavalry, who married Margaret Grant of Bught, with an only child Margaret, who died young. Much sympathy was felt for Mrs. Macqueen, who, losing her husband and promising child, bore her losses with christian fortitude.

IX.—John Fraser Macqueen succeeded his brother, Captain Donald; was called to the English bar in 1838, and appointed Queen's Counsel and Bencher in 1861. He held a legal appointment, and was considered an authority on certain branches of the law. His elder brother, Hugh, W.S., was a man of great ability, whose untimely end created a great sensation in Edinburgh and the North. John Fraser Macqueen died on 6th December, 1881, having resided in England for about fifty years. After his death the succession to the headship, but not to the estate, opened to his only surviving brother, last surviving son of Captain Donald Macqueen the VII.,

X.—Lachlan, the ninth and youngest son, a distinguished officer in the service of the East India Company, who died in 1896. This worthy gallant officer, whom I had the pleasure of seeing at his home in Devonshire, shortly before his death, had, notwithstanding his long residence abroad, a wonderful and minute knowledge of the history of his own and other Northern families. Indeed his absence from the North only served to intensify his attachment and recollections for persons and events in his boyhood. During his long and honourable career in India he became intimately acquainted with most of the numerous and illustrious Scotsmen of his day, those who were the foremost in keeping with enthusiasm all the clannish feelings and aims of the race. As he knew I was a collector of old papers, he asked my sympathy while narrating that many old and valuable family papers which remained with the family, and had been carefully preserved by each succeeding generation, were wantonly burnt and destroyed by an Englishwoman, into whose hands they fell, knowing it would vex and distress him.

Colonel Macqueen was survived by his wife and several children, his only son

XI.—Donald, now resident in New Zealand, present representative of the Macqueens of Corrybrough, whose portrait, when in the army, is given.

DONALD MACQUEEN OF CORRYBROUGH.

Macqueens of Pollochaig, Clune, Strathnoon.

Next in importance to Corrybrough was the family of Macqueen of Pollochaig. This estate, in Strathdearn, fell into the hands of The Mackintosh towards the close of last century. The Pollochaig Macqueens are said to have been in the place for three hundred years, and up to the time of John Macqueen, who lived in the early part of last century, prospered. It is reported of this John that he possessed supernatural powers, and by means of certain candles which he framed, was able to look into and behold the unseen. His mistake in not demanding a blessing from the witch he had shot, under guise of a roe, before extracting at her request the leaden bullet, I have told elsewhere at length, and is indeed well known. But the wording of the blessing, which he did not ask until after he had extracted the bullet, was so peculiar and distressing that it may be here given, viz. :—" That his (Macqueen's) worst day would be his best day, and his best day his worst day." From and after this pronunciamento, the family decayed. John Macqueen's position may be inferred from the circumstance that his son, Donald, married Elizabeth, sister of Lachlan Mackintosh of Mackintosh, and in consequence of his being "out" as one of the officers of the regiment of Clan Chattan in 1715, was banished to the plantations of America, leaving at least one daughter, Elizabeth Macqueen. Several of these Macqueens remained about the place as late as 1825—1835, when the late Mr. S. F. Mackintosh of Farr was framing his histories.

I mention the names of such families as have been noted at different periods.

Of the family of Raigmore I mention in the year 1697 Duncan Macqueen, Portioner of Raigmore, alias Meikle Raig, and Marie Cunningham, his spouse, James Macqueen, their son, and Elizabeth Dallas, his spouse. In 1701-1721 Donald Macqueen of Clune and Isobel Mackintosh, his present spouse, are mentioned, and in 1724 their son, William Macqueen. In 1749 Lachlan, son of William, and grandson of Donald of Clune, is mentioned. In 1783 the minor branches of Corrybrough held a davoch of land in Strathdearn, viz. :— Strathnoon, 1 plough; Clune, 2 ploughs; Easter Raigmore, 1 plough; the whole paying a feu to the Earl of Moray of £3 0s. 6½d., and now forming part of the estate of Balnespick. The feu of Corrybrough is £13 19s.

Pleasing reminiscences connected with the Corrybrough family, extending over a hundred years, hang around Donald Fraser, blacksmith at Moy Hall, hero in 1746 of the "Rout of Moy," so well known and frequently described, otherwise the defeat of Lord Loudon and his host by Donald Fraser and his few men, known in Gaelic as "Captain of the Five." Donald Fraser's name is still held in high honour, exciting the admiration of Highlanders in no ordinary degree.

Donald Fraser was, I am informed, born on Corrybrough estate, to which locality he removed in his later years, and he and his descendants have ever since, so far as necessary, been nourished and protected by the Corrybrough family

MINOR SEPTS OF CLAN CHATTAN.   79

Mr. S. F. Mackintosh, in his collections of 1835, gives a full account of the rout, and observes "that there are several

SWORD OF DONALD FRASER,
Hero of the Rout of Moy.

descendants of Fraser still living at Moymore and Corrybrough, of the names of Leslie and Fraser."

In a list of the officers of Clan Chattan killed at Culloden, taken from the papers of Lord George Murray,

TOMBSTONE OF DONALD FRASER.
In Moy Churchyard.

Donald Fraser is mentioned as one, but if the tradition be true that only three officers escaped, there is some doubt on the point. The three who escaped were Alexander Mackintosh, younger son of Essich, greviously wounded, Duncan Mackintosh, younger son of Mackintosh of Corrybrough Mor, and Farquhar Macgillivray, younger of Dalcrombie. Donald Fraser's grandson, also Donald, during a long life was closely attached to the Macqueens, for whom he had that admiration, fidelity, and respect, so characteristic of the old Highlanders. It was affectingly said of him :—" If you want to put a smile on Donald Fraser's face, talk about Captain Macqueen and family." This Donald Fraser's widow, of great age, is still alive, as also her daughter Miss Jane, who after a long and useful career in England has settled with her mother near the abode of Donald Fraser the third, both held in respect by all their neighbours, and in especial by the ladies of the Corrybrough family, daughters of the late Colonel Lachlan Macqueen.

In order to the further preservation of the memory of Donald Fraser, I have caused the following to be engraved:—

1.—Receipt dated 12th December, 1744, signed by him by initials only, as apparently he could not write.

2.—His anvil at Moy Hall, with the words, "Innean Caiptein nan Còig, Domhnull Friseal, 16mh Dara mhios na bliadhna, 1746," which may be translated—Anvil, Captain of Five, Donald Fraser, 16th February, 1746.

3.—His sword, preserved with honour in a house in Strathdearn, not indicated by request of the owner, though allowed to be photographed for this work.

L.

4.—His tombstone in the churchyard of Moy, once very handsome, but now by the lapse of time, showing decay in lettering and ornamentation.

Among the numerous Macqueens of the present day who have distinguished themselves may be mentioned Major-General Sir John Withers Macqueen, K.C.B., who entered the Indian Service in 1854, and became Major-General, 10th December, 1892. The bald enumeration of his distinguished services requires sixteen closely printed pages of Hart.

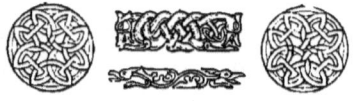

SHAW.

No. V.—THE SHAWS OF ROTHIEMURCHUS.

The various tribes composing the Clan Chattan were by clan historians grouped under two heads—those who, though of a different name, united, associated, and incorporated themselves with and under the Mackintosh as their leader, and those cadets descended of his own house, of old classed under the title of "Fuil 'ic an Tòisich," that is of Mackintosh, his blood. These last were nine in number. The four tribes hitherto dealt with in these papers, viz: Macgillivrays, Macbeans, Macphails, and Macqueens had all voluntarily associated themselves, and fell under the first class above noted.

In the case of the Shaws, they, like the Farquharsons, were both of the class second, above noted, being descended of Mackintosh, his house; in course of time, however, they became leaders of their own sept and assumed a distinctive surname.

The name of Shaw became numerous, and is both powerful and influential at the present day, and while it is not asserted or claimed that every Shaw is necessarily of Clan Chattan, the clan is most willing to welcome all and every Shaw disposed to come in, and adhere to the connection.

In Sir Eneas Mackintosh's History he places the Shaws

second of the nine cadets of his own house (the Toshes of Monyvaird being first), and gives

I.—the descent of the first Shaw of Rothiemurchus as son of Gilchrist, son of John, son of Angus, 6th Mackintosh, and it is generally admitted that Shaw commanded the thirty of Clan Chattan at the North Inch of Perth in 1396, in absence of his chief, incapacitated by age. From the configuration of his front teeth Shaw was called *Corr fiachlach*, and for his valour and success in 1396 was put in possession, though without written title, of the lands of Rothiemurchus, which lands had been held by the Mackintoshes of and under the Bishops of Moray since the year 1236. Shaw is recorded to have married the daughter of Robert Mac-Alasdair vic Aonas. From and after 1396 Shaw Mackintosh's descendants are understood to have taken the name of Shaw as their surname, but until about 1560 that of Mackintosh adhered, and for some generations the appellation of "Ciar" was also hereditary.

Shaw Mackintosh was interred at Rothiemurchus, and upon his tombstone there were placed eight roughly hewn pebbles, supposed as long as they remained to indicate prosperity to the Shaws. Through lapse of time some of these stones have disappeared, and it is matter of tradition that, although the remaining stones were thrown into the river Spey on more than one occasion by evil-disposed persons, they were miraculously restored. Connected with this ancient grave an outrage was committed a few years ago, by the placing of a tombstone, common-place in design, right over, and covering the ancient one, by some foolish Shaw from America, to the memory of a presumed ancestor, that unfortunate Farquhar Shaw, who, with Samuel and Malcolm Macpherson, suffered death for alleged desertion from the Black Watch, on 18th July, 1743. This belated member of the Clan Shaw confounded Farquhar, who suffered in 1743, with the first Shaw of Rothiemurchus, who died centuries before. The outrage

MODERN TOMBSTONE OVER THE GRAVE OF SHAW MACKINTOSH
OF ROTHIEMURCHUS.

calls for redress by the removal of this piece of falsified history with its misleading inscription, and consequent re-appearance of the ancient memorial now lying below it. The sole object of giving the accompanying illustration, specially prepared for these papers, is to show the small roughly dressed stones. Shaw Mackintosh was succeeded by his son,

II.—James, one of the leading men of Clan Chattan at the battle of Harlaw in 1411, where he fell. This James has been confounded by Boetius with Malcolm Mackintosh, 10th of Mackintosh. In the Kinrara History James is described as "a man highly commended for his valour." He married the daughter of Gregor Grant, leaving two sons, Alisdair, commonly styled "Ciar" or "brown," an epithet which adhered to his successors for generations, and Adam, of whom hereafter under the Shaws of Tordarroch.

III.—Alasdair Ciar being a child at his father's death, the Comyns took the opportunity of re-establishing themselves in Rothiemurchus, and to the Comyns, who were great builders, has to be placed the credit of erecting the well-known castle of Loch-an-Eilean.

The circumstances under which Alasdair Ciar was secreted by his nurse among her friends in Strath Ardil, and her touching recognition of him when he came to manhood by his breathing through the keyhole of the door, the manner of regaining his estate, and the defeat of his enemies at Lag-na-Cnimcineach, are well known, being a favourite ancient story among Highlanders. Alasdair Ciar's predecessors held Rothiemurchus without heritable right, and it was not until 1464 that Alexander obtained his first written title from David Stuart, Bishop of Moray. Alasdair, who married Miss Stuart of Kincardine, is frequently mentioned betwixt the years 1464-1482, and left four sons—John, his successor, Alasdair Og, and James, of whom the Shaws of Dell and Dalnavert respectively, after referred to, and Iver, of whom the Shaws of Harris.

IV.—John, who married Euphemia, daughter of Allan Mackintosh, and grand-daughter of Malcolm, 10th of Mackintosh, with issue;

V.—Allan, who married the fourth and youngest daughter of Farquhar, 13th Mackintosh, by Giles Fraser of Lovat. As early as 1536 Allan is found in pecuniary difficulties, falling into the dangerous hands of the Gordons. The Gordons were unable or unwilling to keep the lands, coveted by the Grants of Grant, and much desired by the Mackintoshes as an important and early possession of the family. The Gordons were willing to deal with Lachlan Mackintosh of Mackintosh, but Grant was too much for him, and acquired Rothiemurchus, greatly to Mackintosh's chagrin, who even condescended to entreat Grant to let him have his family's ancient possession. Here is an excerpt from Mackintosh's letter to Grant, dated 20th February, 1568:—

"And for all these causes above written, and perpetuity of friendship, alliance, and blood, the Laird of Grant whom I esteem my greatest friend, to let me have my own native country of Rothiemurchus for such sums of money as he gave for the same, or as he and I may goodly agree, and that because it is not unknown to the Laird and his wise council that it is my native country as said is."

Having, as might be expected from the family's character, failed in an amicable arrangement, Mackintosh struggled for years to retain forcible possession, but finally, about 1586, had to succumb. Allan's eldest son,

VI.—James, though occasionally found styled of Rothiemurchus, had practically no interest in the estate. His wife bore a name having always unhappy consequences when connected with the Mackintoshes, and her second marriage, with her husband's after behaviour, exciting the ire of her eldest son, Allan Shaw, brought about the downfall of the old house of Rothiemurchus.

The island, with its ruined castle, has attracted the attention of the greatest painters of this century and though much of the grand native forest of pine has disappeared,

LOCH-AN-EILEAN CASTLE.--THE ANCIENT STRONGHOLD OF THE SHAWS OF ROTHIEMURCHUS.

Loch-an-Eilean is still an attractive pilgrimage. There is a remarkable echo from the shore opposite the castle; and it is understood the eagles are now left in peace. A reproduction of a painting in my possession is here given, and I conclude this part of the paper with an account from the Kinrara MS. History of the punishment at Loch-an-Eilean in

1531 of the murderer of Lachlan, the 14th Mackintosh:—

"In revenge of this barbarous murder, Donald Glas Mackintosh (brother's son to the murderer) and Donald Mackintosh Mac.Allan, his cousin, with the assistance of the Laird of Macgregor (brother-in-law to Mackintosh), did within a quarter of a year after the slaughter apprehend the said John Malcolm's son, and incarcerate him in the Isle of Rothiemurchus, where he was kept for a long time in chains, until James, Earl of Moray, then Regent of the Realm, and brother-in-law to Mackintosh, came to the North, in whose presence the said John was beheaded at the south side of the Loch of Rothiemurchus, upon the 1st day of May, 1531."

PART SECOND.—THE SHAWS—TORDARROCH.

Space forbids dealing with the Shaws of Rothiemurchus, the parent stem, after the loss of the estate, but this is of minor importance, as particulars will be found in the valuable works of the late Rev. W. G. Shaw, of Forfar, and Mr. Alexander Mackintosh Mackintosh. I find, however, one of them as late as 1583, when William MacFarquhar vic Iain Ciar renounces to Lachlan Mackintosh of Mackintosh his occupancy of the farm of Ruthven, in Strathdearn. William Shaw could not write, and the renunciation is signed for him by William Cumming, Notary Public, Inverness, at the Isle of Moy, on 6th June, 1583, in presence of John Kerr, burgess of Inverness, Lachlan Macqueen, in Easter Urchill, James Innes, Servitor to Lachlan Mackintosh of Dunachton, Donald MacDoull Macpherson, in Essich, and Gillie Callum Macpherson, Elrig.

Closely connected with Clan Chattan were the Shaws of Tordarroch, otherwise Clan Ay, allied to and forming a prominent part of Clan Chattan so long as clanship was legally recognised. The ancient good feeling still prevails, and has found marked expression in the writings of Mr. Alexander

TORDARROCH FARMHOUSE. (MODERN.)

Mackintosh Mackintosh, formerly Shaw, above referred to, Cadet of Tordarroch.

As already mentioned, the Tordarroch Shaws descend from Adam, son of James, second Shaw of Rothiemurchus. Angus Shaw's grandson,

I.—Angus, settled in Strathdearn about 1468, his posterity

remaining in Tordarroch as wadsetters under Mackintosh for three centuries, and in course of time acquiring in heritage the Davoch of Wester Leys. From the above Adam, the Tordarroch Shaws were styled Clan Ay, a barbarous spelling of the Gaelic Aidh, and down to and including Governor Alexander Shaw, the last possessor of Tordarroch, no tribe of Clan Chattan was more staunch and devoted to the chief than the Shaws of Tordarroch. By the sale of Rothiemurchus, and the outlawry of the son of the last owner, the Rothiemurchus Shaws went down, while the descendants of Adam, the second son of the second Rothiemurchus, were enabled to consolidate themselves, and be recognized in 1609 as one of the Clan Chattan, their head being acknowledged as chieftains of the later Inverness-shire Shaws. Adam was succeeded by his son,

II.—Robert, who was father of Angus and Bean.

III.—Angus is found 1543 a leading man in the clan, but is not designed Shaw, merely Angus Mac Robert. He was the first wadsetter of Tordarroch. Dying without issue, he was succeeded by his brother,

IV.—Bean, or Benjamin, who had two sons, Adam, who succeeded, and Angus, who succeeded his brother, and one daughter, Effie, who married Donald Mac Gillie Callum (Macpherson) of Essich.

V.—Adam Shaw of Tordarroch, known as Ay Mac Bean vic Robert, signs the Bond of Union among the Clan Chattan in 1609, "for himself, and taking the full burden of his race of Clan Ay," establishing, as pointed out by Mr. A. Mackintosh Mackintosh, that the Tordarroch Shaws had by this time attained the position of a distinct sept of Clan Chattan, under their own chieftain. Adam Shaw died 1620-1621, having married Agnes, daughter of Alexander Fraser of Farraline, by whom he left an only daughter, Margaret, married to Donald Mackintosh, lawful son of William Mackintosh of Rayag. He was succeeded by his brother,

TORDARROCH BRIDGE.

VI.—Angus, who, besides Tordarroch, possessed the lands of Knocknagail and Wester Leys. He married Katherine, daughter of Angus Macbean, 1st of Kinchyle. Angus was succeeded by his son,

VII.—Robert, regarding whom there are numerous references during the period 1666-1691. Robert Shaw is one of the subscribers of the Bond given by the Clan Chattan to their chief, Mackintosh, dated Kincairn, 29th November, 1664. By his wife, Agnes Fraser, Robert had, according to Mr. Mackintosh's account, four sons, Alexander, John, Donald, and William, also one daughter, Effie. I find, however, a note of Robert Shaw, younger of Tordarroch, in 1710. Robert Shaw was succeeded by his eldest son,

VIII.—Alexander, who married Anne Mackintosh of Kellachie, and is found during the period 1679-1716. In the rising of 1715 the Clan Chattan put forth nearly all its strength. Alexander himself was too old to take the field, but his son Robert was Captain, another son, Angus, Lieutenant, and his brother, William Shaw, Quartermaster. The conduct of the clan in that memorable rising has been highly commended, and even the Reverend Renegade, Patten, speaks of "their good order and equipment." Another writes, "they were the most resolute and best armed of any that composed the army." Another that the "regiment was reckoned the best the Earl of Mar had." Robert Shaw was taken prisoner at Preston, and died at Newgate, and one of his letters from prison I have the good fortune to possess. John, the youngest son, was a prominent Writer in Inverness, and the confidential adviser of the Mackintosh family. His son William, styled of Craigfield, was possessor of considerable lands in Strathnairn, but his descendants in the male line are extinct.

IX.—Angus Shaw, second son of Alexander Shaw, succeeded his father. Warned by the fate of his elder brother in 1715, and helped by the wit of his wife, Angus did not take a part in the rising of 1745, and was thereby enabled to befriend many of his kin. He was at his house at Wester Leys the day of the battle of Culloden, and thus, unaware of the Prince's hurried call at the old house of Tordarroch, lost the opportunity of ministering to the Prince's wants on his flight to the West, a matter of regret to himself and to his descendants, even to this day. The steep and narrow bridge, near Tordarroch, over which the Prince then rode, still stands, a photo. reproduction of which is given on page 92. Angus married Anne Dallas of Cantray, and of their numerous descendants Mr. Mackintosh Mackintosh gives a full account. His eldest son,

X.—Alexander, commonly known in his late years as "Governor Shaw," from having held the post of Lieutenant Governor of the Isle of Man from 1790 to 1804, succeeded. Governor Shaw had a distinguished military career, chiefly in America, and notwithstanding his early leaving the North, was very clannish and popular with his numerous connections in the Highlands. He married first, Charlotte Stewart of Inverness, and secondly, Anne Elizabeth Blanckley. He had issue by both marriages. Governor Shaw died at Bath in 1811. He was succeeded by his son,

XI.—John Shaw, who also had a distinguished military career, chiefly in India, and died a Major-General in 1835. His portrait is here given. He married Anne Nesbitt, and was succeeded by his eldest son,

MAJOR-GENERAL JOHN SHAW.

XII.—John Andrew, born in 1797, who, after many years' service in India, succeeded in 1842 to the estate of Newhall, in the combined counties of Ross and Cromarty, through his paternal grandmother, adding the name and arms of Mackenzie to his own. Dying without issue, he was succeeded by his nephew.

NEWHALL, ROSS-SHIRE. SEAT OF CHARLES F. H. SHAW-MACKENZIE.

XIII.—Charles Forbes Hodson Shaw, eldest son of Alexander Nesbitt Shaw, second son of John 11th hereof, the present representative of the old Shaws of Tordarroch and Clan Ay. Mr. Shaw-Mackenzie was long a judge in the Bombay Presidency, and his portrait, with a representation of the place of Newhall, are here given. Mr. Shaw-Mackenzie takes a deep interest

CHARLES F. H. SHAW-MACKENZIE.

in his property, and in county affairs, and has lately obtained much and deserved credit by prominently advocating the construction of a railway from Cromarty to connect with the Highland system, thereby developing and opening up that important district of the Black Isle which faces the Cromarty Firth. By his wife, Ellen, daughter of Major General John Ramsay, he had seven sons and two daughters—Vero Kemball, B.A. Cantab, John Alexander, M.D., London, George Malcolm, Charles Frederick Dillon, Arthur Crokat, Grenville Reid, Alexander Nesbitt Robertson (now deceased), Anna Catharine, and Ellen Isabella.

Notwithstanding the downfall of the head family of Rothiemurchus, the name of Shaw became numerous and flourishing in Badenoch, Strathnairn, and the Leys, some branching off to the Black Isle in Ross. Dealing with these branches, I take

Part Three.—I.—The Shaws of Dell.

Sir Robert Sibbald, writing in 1680, speaks of the Shaws as being then numerous, with Alexander Shaw of Dell as their head, acknowledging Mackintosh as their chief, and fighting under his banner. The first Shaw of Dell was

I.—Alasdair Og, second son of Alexander Ciar, 3rd of Rothiemurchus. He was succeeded by his son

II.—James, and he by

III.—Alasdair, who in turn was succeeded by

IV.—Alasdair Og. In 1594, the name of

V.—John Mac Alasdair Og, in Dell, is found, who obtained a heritable right to Dell, his son

VI.—John is infeft in Dell in 1622. This infeftment, which included John's wife, Grizel Stuart of Kineardine, proceeded on disposition by John (No. V.), dated 17th November, 1627, Ferquhard Shaw alias Mac Allister, in Innerie, acts as Bailie, and Alexander Shaw, son of John Shaw, Senior, is one of the witnesses to the infeftment. The last mentioned Alexander Shaw was infeft, 25th July, 1635, in the part of Ghislieh called Cambusmore, on Charter by John Grant of Rothiemurchus; amongst other witnesses to the infeftment are John Shaw, brother-german to Alexander, James Shaw in Dell, James Shaw of Kinrara-na-Coille (otherwise Kinrara of the Woods), Mackintosh's Kinrara. In 1635, I have note of a James Shaw in Dunachton beg, and later on the name spread over the whole parish of Alvie.

The next Shaw of Dell I find is,

VII.—Alexander, in 1681, probably grandson of John VI., as Alexander's son.

VIII.—James Shaw, is mentioned as of full age in 1711, and frequently referred to, up to the year 1758.

James Shaw of Dell was one of the leading men of Clan Chattan, and much trusted and favoured by the Mackintoshes, while he on the other hand was their devoted supporter. He married Marjory Mackintosh of Balnespiek, and had, at least, one son, Alexander, who, prior to 1736, married Anna Mackintosh. In the marriage contract Alexander is designed Younger of Dell. There was no issue of the marriage, as James, the father, was served heir to his son. I am inclined to think that Alexander was one of the officers of the Clan Chattan regiment who fell at Culloden.

I have a deed in 1750 signed by James Shaw, in a feeble hand, which narrates that he, James Shaw of Dell, was then possessor of the Iosal of Dalnavert. The deed is signed at Dalnavert, 8th January, 1750, in presence of Patrick Shaw in Dalnavert, and Angus Shaw of Dalnavert, the writer. Angus Shaw was long Chamberlain over the Mackintosh estates.

Mr. Mackintosh Mackintosh says in his history that James Shaw is the latest Shaw of Dell of whom he has found trace.

FAC-SIMILE OF SIGNATURE OF THE REV. LACHLAN SHAW, THE HISTORIAN.

Of the Shaws of Dell was the well-known Reverend Lachlan Shaw, Historian of Moray. Although Mr. Shaw is not now looked upon as an accurate antiquarian, yet his industry and capacity merit the highest respect. What he had honestly seen, he records clearly and correctly, and as his life (1691-1777) extended over the two risings of 1715 and 1745, he had ample opportunity of observing and recording with accuracy events in the North of exceptional interest and importance. Mr. Shaw was son of Donald Shaw, alias Mac Robert, who resided in Rothiemurchus, and I observe Donald Mac Robert and his son Duncan, get a lease from Mackintosh in 1717 of Achnabechan of Dunachton, with the Reverend Lachlan Shaw as their cautioner. Part of a document with his signature is given on page 99. Mr. Shaw was minister of Kingussie 1716-1719, of Calder 1719-1734, and of Elgin 1734-1774. He demitted in 1774, dying in 1777, in his 86th year. For an account of his descendants reference is made to Mr. Mackintosh Mackintosh's Genealogical Account of the Shaws, pp. 71-72. Inhumanity on the part of Mr. Shaw in connection with the shooting in cold blood of young Kinrara after the battle of Culloden, is hinted at by Robert Chambers, and had some credence. There really never was the slightest foundation for the charge, as the Reverend Lachlan Shaw was at the time minister at Elgin, many miles distant from Culloden. The wrong doer was Mr. Eneas Shaw, then minister of Petty. Mr. James Grant, merchant in Inverness, on the authority of Lachlan Grant, writer in Edinburgh, the original narrator of the story, distinctly charges the inhumanity upon "Mr. Angus Shaw, Presbyterian teacher at Pettie." Bishop Forbes, determined as was his wont to be strictly accurate, wrote to his informant, the Reverend George Innes of Forres, on the subject, who in his reply to the Bishop, under date 29th April, 1750, says, "Mr. Shaw's name is Angus, and not Laughlan, as your gentleman very rightly told you. My mistake proceeded from my thinking upon one Laughlan Shaw, Presbyterian minister at Elgin;" truly a lame excuse.

II.—THE SHAWS OF DALNAVERT.

This family derives from James Shaw, 3rd son of Alexander Ciar, 3rd of Rothiemurchus. They were in Dalnavert from the time of its coming into possession of the Mackintoshes, a part of the Assythment lands obtained from the the Huntly family. Alexander Shaw of Dalnavert is noted, probably grandson of James above noticed, founder of the family. The next Shaw of Dalnavert found is William, noted in 1635-1648. His son Donald is mentioned in 1679 as joining in the Clan Chattan expedition to Lochaber. John Shaw, son of the above Donald, succeeded, and in 1710 Robert Shaw is found. In 1723 Donald, son of the deceased Robert Shaw of Dalnavert, is found, and in 1724-29 Alexander Shaw, younger of Dalnavert. Angus Shaw is next found, long Chamberlain on the Mackintosh estates, many of the family writs being either written or witnessed by him. William, son of Angus, is of full age in 1751, and occupied Dalnavert. Thomas died without issue in 1810, and is interred at Rothiemurchus. William Shaw's daughter, Margaret, married Captain Alexander Clark, of which sept in its order.

In 1791 I find note of Captain James Shaw at Dalnavert, James Shaw in Iosal, Thomas Shaw in Keppoch, Robert Shaw in Rie-Aiteachan, and Thomas Shaw in Rie-nabruaich, both in Glenfeshie.

The Shaws monopolized all Mackintosh's lands east of Feshie River, and the Spey, from Glenfeshie to Rothiemurchus, but at the present day there is only one tenant of the old stock remaining, Mr. John Shaw of Tolvah, on the Feshie.

III.—THE SHAWS OF KINRARA.

John Shaw, styled of Kinrara, was one of the leading men in Badenoch during the first half of the eighteenth century. He was descended of the Shaws of Dalnavert, and married an Aberdeenshire lady, Elizabeth Stewart. He does not appear to have been "out" in 1715, and a permission by General Wade, dated Inverness, 26th August, 1728, allows him to carry arms, his loyalty to the Hanoverian Government being certified by the Lord Advocate and Colonel Farquhar. In 1723 Mackintosh lets to John Shaw, Tackman of Kinrara, his woods in the parish of Alvie. Continuing in favour with his chief, he in 1726 obtains a tack of that part of Dalnavert called Iosal of Croftbeg, and of Achleam-a-choid in Glenfeshie, reserving the portion occupied by Jean Macpherson, relict of John Shaw, sometime of Dalnavert. In 1734 John Shaw gets a new lease of the three ploughs of Kinrara-na-choille, presently possessed by him, and of Rie-na-brnaich in Glenfeshie. Mr. Shaw had three sons, James, Thomas, and John, and two daughters married in Aberdeenshire. James and John Shaw fought at Culloden. Of the latter, already referred to when alluding to the Reverend Lachlan Shaw, the following heart-rending account, from the Jacobite Memoirs, being absolutely authentic, should not be omitted.

THE SLAUGHTER OF SHAW, YR. OF KINRARA, AT CULLODEN.

"The most shocking part of this woful story is still to come—the horrid barbarities committed in cold blood after the battle was over. The soldiers went up and down, knocking on the head such as had any life in them;

and except in a very few instances, refusing all manner of relief to the wounded, many of whom, if properly taken care of, would doubtless have recovered. A little house into which the wounded had been carried was set on fire about their ears, amongst whom was Colonel Orelli, a brave old Irish gentleman in the Spanish service. One Mr. Shaw, yr. of Kinrara, had likewise been carried into another hut, with other wounded men, and amongst the rest a servant of his own, who being only wounded in the arm, could have got off, but chose rather to stay in order to attend his master. The Presbyterian minister at Petty, Mr. Lachlan Shaw (should be Mr. Angus Shaw) being a cousin of Kinrara's, had obtained leave of the Duke of Cumberland to carry off his friend, in return for the good services the said Mr. S. had done the Government, for he had been very active in dissuading his clan and parishioners from joining the Prince, and likewise, as I am told, sent the Duke very pointed intelligence of all the Prince's motions. In consequence of this, on the Saturday after the battle, he went to the place where his friend was, designing to carry him to his own house. But as he came near, he saw an officer's command, with the officer at their head, fire a platoon at fourteen of the wounded Highlanders whom they had taken out of that house, and bring them all down at once; and when he came up he found his cousin, and servant were two of that unfortunate number. I questioned Mr. Shaw himself about the story, who plainly acknowledged the fact, and was indeed the person who informed me of the precise number, and when I asked him if he knew if there were many more murdered that day in the same way, he said he believed there were in all twenty-two."

IV.—SHAWS OR M'AYS OF THE BLACK ISLE.

Some of the Tordarroch Shaws or Clan Ay moved, voluntarily or compulsorily, into Ross-shire about the beginning of the 17th century, settling in particular in and about Taradale. They signed their name "M'Cay" and "Mackay," but had no connection with the Sutherland Mackays. I have some documents early in the 18th century under the hand of Donald M'Cay, Notary Public in Redcastle. The arms on the tombstone in Kilchrist of Duncan M'Ay, dated 1707, clearly show that he was of the blood of Shaw and Mackintosh. Some correspondence on this branch of the Shaws appeared in the Northern newspapers a few years ago, but did not lead to anything. It would be well if some of those specially interested followed out an accurate enquiry into the history of the M'Cays of the Black Isle.

Part Four.—V.—The Shaws of Aberdeen, Perth, and the Isles, etc.

Upon the loss of Rothiemurchus and scattering of the family, the descendants of James Shaw of Tullochgrue,

I.—Allister Roy, son of Achnahatnich, and nephew of Allan Shaw, previously mentioned as 7th and last of Rothiemurchus, come to the front.

II.—James married one of the daughters of Robert Farquharson, first of Invercauld; his elder son, also

III.—James, settled at Crathinard on Deeside, and married his cousin, once removed, the daughter and heiress of John MacHardy of Crathie. His son

IV.—Duncan, the most renowned of his house, was born in 1653, and died in 1726. Duncan was twice married, first to Miss Forbes of Skellater, and secondly to Miss Farquharson of Coldrach. He was Chamberlain to the Earl of Mar, and among other appointments was Captain in the original Black Watch. By his second wife, Duncan had seven sons, James,

John, Donald, Duncan, Allister, Farquhar, and William, also several daughters, one of whom was Grizel, married to Donald Farquharson, grandson of Brouchdearg. As all, except Donald, were married, leaving issue, the descendants of Duncan became very numerous, and to this day there are very many Shaws proud to consider themselves as the offspring of Duncan Shaw of Crathinard. I particularly mention Lieutenant-General David Shaw, Indian Staff Corps (Madras), retired, who claims, and with some reason, to represent Rothiemurchus, being fourth but eldest surviving son of David, third son of David, eldest son of Duncan of Crathinard. This distinguished officer has three sons, the eldest, David George Levinge Shaw, Captain, 1st Punjaub Cavalry, now serving on the East Indian Frontier, and one surviving brother, Doyle Money Shaw, Deputy Inspector of Hospitals, C.B., for services at the Siege of Alexandria, with medals for the Crimea, China, and Abyssinia.

Five of Duncan's sons, viz., John, Donald, Allister, Farquhar, and William, were all out in the '45. For an account of Duncan's family, (styled himself "Reim aon," or the man of power), reference is made to the late Rev. W. G. Shaw's work, he having been great-grandson of Duncan of Brouchdearg above mentioned, the fourth son of Duncan of Crathinard. About 1710, Crathinard, having met with severe losses, had to sell his estate, which was purchased by Invercauld. He then removed to Glenisla, where he rented Crandard from the Earl of Airlie. His circumstances improving, Duncan wished to buy Crathinard back, but Invercauld would not part with it. This embittered Duncan's latter days, and forced him to remain in Glenisla, where he died, his grave being still pointed out. A *fac-simile* of General Hugh Mackay's license to Crathinard to carry arms, dated 26th June, 1690, is now given. It may be noted here that Crandard was long the possession of the MacComies, also a branch of Clan Chattan. Through V.—Duncan Shaw, of Balloch in Glenisla, fourth son of Crathinard, who was twice married, first to Miss Small of Dirnanean, and secondly to Miss Farquharson of Coldach, descended, with others, the family of whom the present Mr. Duncan Shaw, W.S., of Inverness, is a member, and as Mr. Shaw's family have again settled in Inverness-shire, where for nearly a century they have held honourable position, some account of Mr. Shaw's predecessors is given. Duncan Shaw of Balloch, fourth son of Duncan of Crathinard, both before mentioned, had four sons and two daughters, of whom it is only necessary to mention his third son,

FAC SIMILE OF CRATHINARD'S LICENSE.

VI.—William Shaw, who became proprietor of Dalnaglar, in Glenshee. William's eldest son,

VI.—Duncan, sold Dalnaglar and left the district, having,

about 1810, been appointed Sheriff Substitute of Skye. Duncan married Anne, eldest daughter of Kenneth Macleod of Ebost, and through his grandmother's family Mr. Duncan Shaw has inherited the valuable Prince Charlie relics, more particularly after referred to, and which he has kindly allowed to be copied for this work. After a residence of some years in Skye, Sheriff Duncan Shaw was transferred to the Long Island district of Inverness-shire, at same time filling the offices of factor to Lord Macdonald in North Uist, to Clanranald in South Uist, to Macneill of Barra, and on the estate of Harris. Sheriff Duncan Shaw resided at Nunton of Benbecula, and while there, had the honour of entertaining Marshal Macdonald, Duke of Tarentum. This distinguished soldier was highly pleased with his reception in the Isles, and it is recorded that he was greatly taken with the beauty of one of the sisters-in-law of his host, Miss Macleod of Ebost, who happened to be at Nunton at the time. When South Uist was sold, Sheriff Shaw removed to North Uist, to Sponish, near Lochmaddy, where he died in 1844. Duncan Shaw was succeeded by his only son,

VIII.—Charles, who in his youth, passing as Writer to the Signet, was appointed Chamberlain to Lord Macdonald at Portree, and afterwards settled in the Long Island, over which he was Sheriff-Substitute for forty years. After a long and honourable career, Sheriff Charles Shaw demitted office and took up his residence at Inverness, where he died in 1885. He married Anne, eldest daughter of James Thomas Macdonald, of Balranald, a family of long standing in Uist, leaving

108   MINOR SEPTS OF CLAN CHATTAN.

IX.—Duncan Shaw, and several other sons and daughters. Mr. Duncan Shaw is a member of one of the largest territorial

PRINCE CHARLIE RELICS

and mercantile legal firms in the North, fills various public offices, and is an enthusiastic volunteer.

The knife, fork, and spoon (engraved), were in Prince Charles' daily use after the battle of Culloden and his wanderings in the Isles, and on 3rd July, 1746, were presented by him to Dr. Murdoch Macleod of Eyre, younger son of

MEDALLION OF MARIE
CLEMENTINA SOBIESKI.

OBVERSE OF THE
SOBIESKI MEDALLION.

PORTRAIT OF PRINCE CHARLIE.

the 8th Macleod of Raasay. Dr. Macleod gave them to his daughter, Miss Anne Macleod, and she presented this and other relics to her great-nephew, Sheriff Charles Shaw, and they now belong to his eldest son, the present Mr. Duncan

Shaw. Prince Charles' portrait was given to Dr. Macleod at the same time by the Prince. The gold encasement was afterwards obtained by Dr. Macleod. The medallion of the Prince's mother, Marie Clementina Sobieski, was at the same time given. Mr. Shaw's sisters, in answer to enquiries connected with this book, mention that they frequently heard their grandmother, Mrs. Duncan Shaw, a lady of singular acuteness and reliability, mention the facts connected with her grandfather Eyre coming into the possession of these valuable relics. Mr. Shaw married, in 1889, Elizabeth, daughter of George Gordon, Esq., and his eldest daughter, Katherine Douglas Gordon, born in 1889, is 9th in descent from James Shaw of Tullochgrue, nephew of the last Shaw of Rothiemurchus.

The descendants of Iver, youngest son of Alasdair, 3rd of Rothiemurchus, who removed to the Isles, taking root in the Hebrides, became numerous. I may refer to one family, that of Mr. Alexander Shaw, an influential merchant, banker, and magistrate of Inverness towards the close of last century. When the Macleod estates were being broken up, the Barony of Waternish was acquired by Bailie Shaw. He was succeeded by his son, James Shaw, who was also proprietor of Muirtown and Woodside in the County of Ross. Failing in his circumstances, all James Shaw's property had to be sold.

Of the Irish Shaws of Clan Chattan, the present Sir Robert Shaw and his brothers hold high positions. Sir Robert is descended of Sir Frederick, brother of Sir Robert, son of Sir Robert Shaw, first Baronet. The first Sir Robert was son of Robert, second son of Captain William Shaw, of General Ponsonby's Regiment, *temp*, William III. These Shaws, notwithstanding their long residence in Ireland, are very clannish.

The name of Shaw is numerous and influential in America. I understand upwards of three thousand heads of families are to be found in States' Directories. Let the Shaws close up, and again becoming a power in the North, allow the *Bodach an Dune* to rest in peace.

> Loch-an Eilean, sad and lone,
> Long has thy day of pride been gone;
> Rothiemurchus knows no more
> The race that dwelt upon thy shore;
> Scattered now in every clime
> Waiting the appointed time,
> When they shall return to thee—
> *Fide et Fortudine.**
> Yes, Loch-an-Eilean to thy shore
> Shall the Shaws draw nigh once more,
> And with a joy inspiring strain
> Behold the Shaws arise again.

* The motto of the Shaws.

No. VI.—THE CLARKS.

Sir Eneas Mackintosh places the Clarks or Clan Chlerich No. 12 of Clan Chattan, and says that they, with the Macleans of the North, the Macqueens, and the Clan vic Gillandrish of Connage, took protection for themselves and posterity, of Mackintosh about 1400. Kinrara in his history thus refers to their joining the Clan Chattan—"Sicklike also Gillie Michael vic Chlerich, of whom the Clan Chlerich had their denomination, lived in this Malcolm's time."

Unfortunately the Clarks, who dwelt chiefly in and about Inverness, and in the Lordships of Pettie, Strathdearn and Badenoch, did not, so far as I have observed, own lands, consequently their early and even latter history is necessarily rather obscure. The name Clark shows an undoubted ecclesiastical derivation, strengthened by its form in Gaelic, Chlerich. As the distinguished Irish race of O'Clery was closely allied to, and of the race of Chlerich, a brief account of them may be given.

While as a rule totally opposed to Highlanders having a Norman or Irish extraction foisted upon them, I am glad, in the case of the Clarks, to recognise in the O'Clerys a distinguished branch of the Chlerichs.

Scotsmen have been accused of pride in ancestry, and of framing fictitious descents, and ascents going back to the Flood. The Campbell and Urquhart genealogies do not err on the side of modesty, but may be termed truly so when contrasted with some Irish genealogies. In the O'Shaughnessy pedigree it is gravely stated that Feargall, 96th of his house, was ancestor of O'Cleirigh, and MacCleirigh anglicized O'Clery, Cleary, Clark, Clarke, and Clarkson; but it was not until the time of the 106th of his line that we arrive at Congallach O'Clery, who first assumed this surname, and died 1025. From Shane the elegant, 116th of the line, and from his brothers Donald, Thomas, and Cormac, are descended the O'Chlerys of Tyrconnel, O'Chlerys of Tyrawley in Mayo, the O'Chlerys of Brefney-O'Reilly, and the O'Chlerys of County Kilkenny. The princely residence of the O'Chlerys was at the Castle of Kilbarron in Donegal, and of it and its occupants the late Dr. Petrie says: "This lonely insulated fortress was erected as a safe and quiet retreat in troublous times for the laborious investigators and preservers of the history, poetry, and antiquities of their country. This castle was the residence of the Ollamhs, bards, and antiquarians of the people of Tyrconnell, the illustrious family of the O'Chlerys."

A well known Irish annalist in giving a list of the Irish chiefs and clans in the 12th century, under No. 19, writes: "O'Clery or Clark, hereditary historians of the O'Donnels, and the learned authors of the Annals of the Four Masters and other works on Irish history and antiquities. They had

P

large possessions in the Barony of Tir Hugh, and resided in their Castle of Kilbarron, the ruins of which still remain on a rock on the shore of the Atlantic near Ballyshannon."

Again it is said that O'Clery or Clark was a branch of the O'Clerys of Connaught and Donegal, and of the same stock as the compilers of the "Annals of the Four Masters."

I am indebted to Mr. Andrew Clark, Solicitor, Leith, for much of the foregoing information. He informs me that the materials for his history of the Clarks, extending to over a thousand pages, with two hundred and fifty illustrations, the labour of years, is now, by the desire of the Roman Catholic Bishop of Clogher, in the hands of an Irish Professor of Theology, preliminary to its publication. I trust that this valuable work may soon see the light. As regards Clark tartan, Mr. Andrew Clark writes "that he is not aware of any, in which he is corroborated by his uncle, Mr. Peter Clark, resident in Monaghan, aged ninety, very intelligent and conversant with the traditions of the sept." Mr. Clark has kindly allowed his coat of arms to be given.

I observe the name of Clark connected with the North for the first time in 1456, when Sir Andrew Clark, Chaplain, within the diocese of Moray, is mentioned. In 1492 William Clark is one of the assessors in a perambulation of disputed marches in Aberchirder, twixt Alexander Innes of that ilk, and Alexander Symson, Vicar of Aberchirder. In 1506 John Clark sits as a juror on an inquest regarding certain lands in Nairnshire. In 1522-24-44 and 1557 William Clark is mentioned acting in the same capacity, regarding lands in the parish of Rafford, and lands near the river Lossie in Moray.

During the last two hundred years the name connected with the church is found in and about Inverness. One of the oldest memorials in the chapelyard of Inverness is to the memory of one of the clergy of Inverness, Alexander Clark, and to his wife, a lady of rank. In the same place is buried the Rev. Alexander Clark, a man of great weight and power in my early days. Several Clarks held high municipal and legal honours; and of Alexander Clark, Sheriff-Substitute at Inverness, descended Mr. James Clark, long resident in Italy before the French Revolution, who made certain bequests to Inverness, the place of his nativity.

Although the Clarks held no land, and therefore difficult to trace out, it would appear that they spread over Petty, and to Strathdearn and Badenoch. The Rev. Alexander Clark, born in Petty, was long a schoolmaster there, with a high reputation. He married one of the aunts of Provost John Mackintosh of Aberarder, and settled in a parish in the Hebrides. His letters, however, indicate a strong affection to his native district of Petty. Mr. Clark's reputation as a teacher brought him the sons of important gentlemen as boarders, and amongst those boarded with him in the spring of 1746 were Alexander Baillie, 4th of Dochfour, the Honourable Archibald Fraser of Lovat, and James Mackintosh of Farr. The whole district of Culloden was in a state of agitation on the 16th of April, 1746. If the Petty school met on that unhappy day, it broke up early, and as the attraction of the firing of cannons proved irresistible, most of the scholars, including the three boys above mentioned, straggled towards the field. The brother of one, and the father of another were engaged, and it was a miracle the boys escaped. Alexander Baillie above mentioned was born in 1734, one hundred and sixty four years ago, yet one of his nieces is still alive (1898).

In Badenoch, as early as 1625, the names of John Mac Andrew vic Chlerich, Donald Mac Iain vic Chlerich, and Duncan Mac Iain vic Chlerich, tenants and dependants of Mackintosh, are found. In 1763 Andrew Clark and Alexander Clark, both in Dallanach, parish of Kingussie, are noted. An important man in Badenoch in his day was John Clark, Baron Bailie to the Duke of Gordon. Mr. Clark had two sons, one Captain Alexander Clark, some time of Knappach, afterwards of Invernahaven. After the Shaws left Dalnavert, the place was for a considerable time occupied by Captain James Clark. The last Clark in Dalnavert died within the memory of people still living, and was highly complimented in the New Statistical Account of Scotland for his great improvements as an agriculturist. One of Captain Clark's daughters married Mr. Macdonald, Sanside, and was mother of the celebrated Canadian Statesman the late Sir John A. Macdonald. Another of the Badenoch Clarks was the well known Mr. Alexander Clark, Writer in Ruthven, whose grand-daughter, the late Mrs. Robertson of Benchar, the last of her race, died without issue in 1896. All the Clarks of Inverness, Petty, Strathdearn, and Badenoch were of Clan Chattan. The name at the present day is numerous and influential in the army, medicine, diplomacy and otherwise. In particular Sir Thomas Clark, showing a good example, is one of the most influential and heartiest members of the Edinburgh Clan Chattan Association. The publishing firm in Edinburgh of Messrs. Clark, from which Sir Thomas Clark, Bart., has lately retired, has been eminent in the Capital for nearly a century. Thomas Clark, grandfather of Sir Thomas, was born in the parish of Latheron in Caithness, but settled in Edinburgh, which became the permanent residence of the family. His son John Clark, father of Sir Thomas, became one of the Magistrates of Edinburgh. Another son, Thomas, founded in 1821 the great publishing business, and amongst the thousands upon thousands of volumes published or belonging to the firm, there is perhaps none so honoured and cherished as the well-worn Gaelic bible, used by Thomas the first. Sir Thomas Clark, besides having filled various important offices, was Lord Provost of Edinburgh, 1885-88. His sons, Major John Maurice Clark, and Thomas George Clark, are the present partners of the house.

The time is favourable for the Clarks, now so numerous and influential,—including six baronets,—and the MacChlerichs, more closely uniting, associating and incorporating themselves, with and unto the Clan Chattan, as did their predecessors in 1400. They will be heartily received.

No. VII.—THE GOWS—Sliochd Gow Crom.

The Gows are placed by Sir Eneas Mackintosh No. 8 of the associated tribes of Clan Chattan, and he adds that they took protection of Mackintosh, anno 1399.

While it is likely to remain an open question who were the opponents of Clan Chattan at the fight on the North Inch of Perth in 1396, it is universally admitted that one of the combatants on the victorious side was an armourer or smith, some say a saddler, in Perth. This combatant took the part of an absent sick man when the thirty combatants on either side were mustered. During the five hundred years that have since elapsed this memorable fight stands prominently out.

Clan and other historians are full of the details, but curiously vague as to one of the parties, sometimes Clan Quele, on other occasions Clan Cay. When I come to the Davidsons, I propose dealing with the point, passing on at present to that noble volunteer immortalized in the Fair Maid of Perth. According to one of the Clan Chattan chroniclers:—

"When it was found that one of the combatants was absent through having fallen sick, it was at first proposed to balance the difference by withdrawing one, but no one could be prevailed to quit the danger. In this emergency one Henry Wynd, brought up in the hospital (that is free Educational Seminary) at Perth, commonly called 'An Gow Crom,' *i.e.* the crooked or bandy legged smith, offered to supply the sick man's place for a French crown of gold about three half crowns in sterling money, a great sum in those days. [Here I interpose in the narrative by a short quotation from another MS. history —'Henry of the Wynd, a spectator of the muster, being sorry that so notable a fight should fail, offered to supply the place of the sick man.'] The smith, being an able swordsman, contributed much to the glory of the day, and in the end ten men of Clan Chattan, including the smith, remained, all grieviously wounded, while of their opponents all were killed with the exception of one, who, throwing himself into the River Tay, escaped."

It is related "that so soon as the smith had killed his man he sat down and rested, merely defending himself if attacked. His Captain, sore pressed, asking the reason was told that he, the smith, had performed his engagement, and by killing an opponent had earned his wages. Whereupon the Captain begged the smith to continue the fight for which he would be amply rewarded, over and above the stipulated wage, to which the smith replied in words of such singular significance, that they have ever since been proverbial, and are destined to last as long as the Gaelic language endures:

"Am fear nach cunndadh rium, cha chunndainn ris."
Which may be rendered
"He who keeps no account of his good deeds to me, I will repay without measure,"
and re-engaging in the strife, contributed greatly to the success of his side.

The happy connection betwixt Henry Smith, and the Clan Chattan, was not destined to terminate with the fight. Henry was invited to the north, and to unite with the clan for the future,—and it is recorded that "Henry of the Wynd set out from Perth, with a horse load of his effects, and said he would not take up his residence or habitation until his

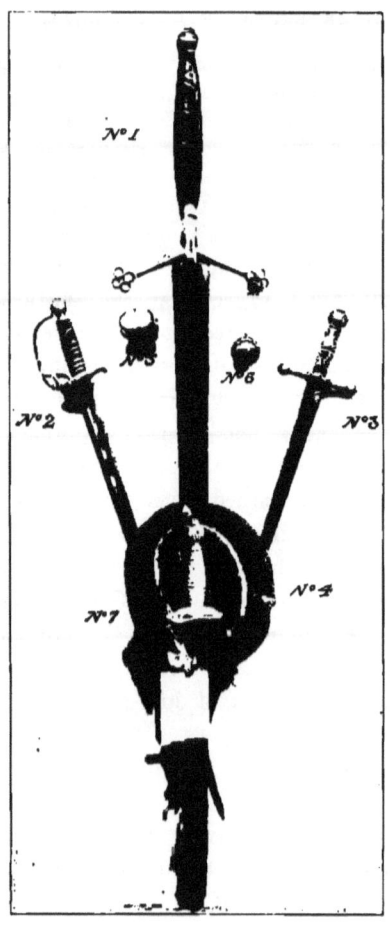

HISTORICAL RELICS IN THE POSSESSION
OF MACKINTOSH OF MACKINTOSH, MOY HALL.

No. 1. Ancient *Claidheamh Mòr* (Claymore) used at the Battle of the North Inch of Perth A.D. 1396. No. 2. Viscount Dundee's Sword, with which he fought at Killiecrankie. No. 3. Sword given to Lachlan Mackintosh by Charles I. No. 4. Sword given to the Chief of Mackintosh by Pope Leo IX. No. 5. Snuff Mull which belonged to James V. No. 6. Watch of Mary Queen of Scots. No. 7. Prince Charlie's Bonnet, left by him at Moy Hall, February, 1746.

load fell, which happened in Strath Avon in Banffshire, where he accordingly settled. The place is called to this day Leac-a'-Ghobhainn. The Smiths or Gows, and Mac-Glashans are commonly called 'Sliochd a' Ghobha Chrom,' but all agree that he had no posterity, though he had many followers of good position to the number of twelve, who were proud of being reputed the children of so valiant a man. The more to ingratiate themselves in his favour, they generally learned to make swords as well as to use them. His twelve followers spread themselves over the country, in time, many assuming the name of Mackintosh, their chief."

In 1589 the name of Thomas Gow, nottar, is found to a Bond by Keppoch to Mackintosh, signed at Dunkeld.

Many of the leading Gows settled in the Parish of Alvie. James Gow is tenant under Mackintosh in Badenoch in 1635, and in 1679 the names of William Gow and Ewen Gow, in Crathiecroy of Laggan, are noted. In the rising of 1745 the name of Alexander Gow in Ruthven is found, a private in the Jacobite Army, regarding whom a Hanoverian guager bearing the appropriate name of Campbell was pleased to report that he "insulted the country people."

Coming down to recent times, the Gows are now chiefly east of Spey, on the banks of Feshie. Some of them possess great musical talent, worthy of their celebrated namesake, Neil Gow, who may have been himself of Clan Chattan. Others have shown literary powers, and one head-keeper at Dunachton possessed some of the skill and characteristics of a Red Indian hunter.

As the Gows, like the Clarks, had no lands in the north, they in like manner are difficult to trace. But I will refer to one, to whom Highlanders are much indebted. Mr. John Gowie, retired officer of Excise, whom I knew very well, a native of Strathdearn, occupied himself much in his well-earned retirement, being a skilful draughtsman, in framing an elaborate plan of the battlefield of Culloden and its surroundings. The field as now viewed, with its great reclamations and plantations, can give no visitor a correct idea of what the place was in 1746. In Mr. Gowie's plan, framed when matters were much in the same position as for the previous hundred years, he was able to identify the position of the armies, the different regiments and clans, and their numbers, with an accuracy and fulness of detail now impossible to equal. Contrasted with this plan, those made at the time, and even the later plan prepared for Home's history, are mere daubs. Here I would like to say that since Mr. Gowie's time, other retired officers of Excise in the north, such as Mr. A. Carmichael and Mr. John Murdoch, have greatly opened up and illustrated Highland matters, deservedly earning the respect and gratitude of their Highland countrymen.

DAVIDSON.

No. VIII.—THE DAVIDSONS, OR CLAN DHAI.

ARMS OF DAVIDSON OF CANTRAY.

Sir Eneas Mackintosh places the Davidsons 4th of Clan Chattan, and states that they associated themselves with, and took protection of and under William Mackintosh, 7th of Mackintosh, prior to 1350.

Kinrara in his history unfortunately does not refer to the incorporation, but mentions that "the Davidsons, styled of Invernahaven in Badenoch, were, according to common tradition, originally a branch of the Comyns." After the Comyns' downfall, Donald dhu of Invernahaven associated himself with the Clan Chattan, then rapidly rising into power, and having married Sloan, daughter of Angus, 6th Mackintosh, became a leading member of Clan Chattan, and was received with such favour by the Captain, as to excite the jealousy of another tribe. This jealousy brought about the virtual extinction of the Davidsons.

The Davidsons, known as Clan Dhai, from their first known leader, David dhu of Invernahaven, were chief actors in the two notable fights at Invernahaven and the North Inch of Perth, and the losers in both battles under the name of Clan Dhai. This name, Dhai, at first barbarously given as "Cay," and afterwards excruciatingly rendered into "Quele" by Scottish scribes ignorant of the Gaelic language, for a long time puzzled historians; but that the Davidsons, or

From R. Ronald M'Ian's]   DAVIDSON.   [*"Clans of the Scottish Highlands."*

Clan Dhai, formed one of the combatants is not questioned at the present day by any competent authority.

Assuming, as reasonable, that the Davidsons, who had hitherto followed the banner of the predominant Comyns, were unwilling to yield to any other than the Captain of Clan Chattan, their new chief and near connection, the bitter antagonism to the pretensions of another tribe of Clan Chattan becomes intelligible. The Davidsons and Macphersons were both not only of Clan Chattan, but the chief's relatives. Whatever the cause, the feud became so keen as to extend beyond the power of the Captain of Clan Chattan or that of the Earls of Crawford and Moray, deputed by the King to pacify them. So the feud straggled on, and was not terminated until 1396, at the battle of the North Inch of Perth, when all the Davidsons, probably leading men, were killed except one, whereby the family sunk.

Dealing with the battle at Invernahaven—a beautiful district at the junction of the rivers Truim and Spey, where there was a ford, hence the name, now, alas, under a comparatively recent ownership, ruined and neglected, an uninhabited waste— I proceed to refer to the battle, quoting from a MS. of the early part of this century, the writer having been an educated and reliable antiquarian. He says :—

"A considerable part of the Mackintosh's estate lying in Lochaber, distant from his residence, had for convenience been let to the Camerons, a neighbouring clan, and by their refusing to pay the stipulated rent Mackintosh was often obliged to seize their cattle, when several fights occurred betwixt them with varying success.

About the year 1370 the Camerons convened their numerous clan and dependents together, with such others as they could prevail upon to assist them— such as Campbells and Macdonalds— to make reprisals. Mackintosh knowing their intention soon collected an equal force, consisting also of several tribes, under the general name of Clan Chattan to oppose them. But when the armies came in sight, an unreasonable difference arose betwixt two of these tribes, viz., the Macphersons and Davidsons. Though they both agreed that Mackintosh should command the whole as Captain of Clan Chattan, yet they could not agree who should have the right hand of the other. Macpherson contended for it as chief of his clan, and Davidson as being head of another branch of Clan Chattan equally ancient. This dispute being referred to Mackintosh, he imprudently decided in favour of Davidson of Invernahaven, which gave such offence to the Macphersons, that Cluny drew off his men, who stood idle spectators, while the Mackintoshes, Davidsons, and others, becoming, by this withdrawal, overpowered by numbers, were defeated."

Here I interpose in the narrative to mention that Mackintosh drew off his men towards Strath-na-Eilich, in the parish of Laggan, and encamped for the night at a spot where a streamlet running north-east falls into the Eilich, as does the Eilich into the Spey, and the streamlet is known to this day as Alt-Rie-an-Toishich. The narrative goes on to say:

"That Mackintosh, being irritated and disappointed by the behaviour of the Macphersons, sent at nightfall his own bard, as if he came from the Camerons, to the camp of the Macphersons to provoke them to fight, by repeating the following satyrical lines in Gaelic, which now handed down orally for upwards of five hundred years, is a noted instance of the vitality of many old Gaelic 'says' connected with the Clan Chattan:—

> Tha luchd na foille air an tom,
> Is am Balg-shuilich donn na dhraip—
> Cha b'e bhur càirdeas ruinn a bh'ann
> Ach bhur lamh a bhi cho tais.

Which may be translated.—

The false party are on the field beholding their chief in danger; it was not your love for us that made you abstain from fighting, but merely your own cowardice.

This reproach so stung Macpherson, that, calling up his men, he attacked the Camerons that same night in the camp, and made a dreadful slaughter of them, and pursuing them to the foot of a mountain, killed their chief, Charles MacGillony, at a place called to this day 'Corrie Tearlaich,' or Charles' Valley.

Though the above conflict put an end to the dispute with the Camerons for the time, yet it created another equally dangerous betwixt the Macphersons and the Davidsons. Those were perpetually plundering and killing each other, in so much that the King sent Lindsay, Earl of Crawford, and Dunbar, Earl of Moray, two of the greatest noblemen in this kingdom, to compromise matters and reconcile them. This being found impossible to do without bloodshed, gave rise to the celebrated trial of valour on the North Inch of Perth, which happened on Monday before the feast of St. Michael, in the time of Robert the 3rd, anno 1396."

In dealing with the Shaws, I have already sufficiently referred to this great fight, and now only mention that from this date the Davidsons were practically so broken up, that for centuries they never regained a recognised position. Having no land, the name cannot be clearly traced. Kinrara in his history makes the following comment on the battle:—

"After the fight, the Clan Chattan gave a new heritable bond of service and manrent to Lachlan Mackintosh, their chief, because they had prospered so well under the happy conduct of his cousin Shaw, and Lachlan gave to Shaw possession of the lands of Rothiemurchus for the valour he had shown that day against the enemies."

In my youth, I recollect of hearing a Gaelic bard run over the tribes of Clan Chattan, but have never been able, in despite of varied enquiries, to get a copy of his verses. All I recollect is that the Tordarroch Shaws and the Davidsons followed each other, thus: "Clan Ay agus Clan Dhai."

The Davidsons, presently in Inverness-shire, are mainly to be found in the parishes of Dores, Inverness, and Petty, and in the districts of Strathnairn, Strathdearn, and Badenoch. Two clergymen, the Rev. Mr. Davidson of Lochalsh, and the late worthy minister of the Free Church in South Harris, are of Clan Chattan, and the name is rapidly rising in importance.

Two prominent families—the Davidsons of Cantray, in Inverness, and of Tulloch, in Ross—came to the front much about the same time—during the last half of the eighteenth century—and there is no reason why the Davidsons, so numerous and influential in the South of Scotland and in England, should not unite with their Northern brethren and choose a leader, say Cantray or Tulloch, both true Highlanders, young and ambitious men. The talented and energetic Secretary of the Clan Chattan Association of Glasgow should see to this, and thereby greatly add to his good work in the consolidation of Clan Chattan.

No. IX.—THE MACLEANS OF THE NORTH.
Clan Thearlaich.

Dochgarroch.

Sir Charles Maclean, of the family of Duart, having been appointed Governor of the Royal Castle of Urquhart on the west side of Loch Ness, he and his posterity took up their abode in the North, and were known as the Macleans of the North, and afterwards of Dochgarroch. During his life, Sir Charles maintained his position, and as a matter of tradition, it is stated that he built Castle Spiritan, (sometimes Castle Spirital), at the foot of Loch Ness, of which the view, fortunately preserved, and in my possession, by an amateur taken early in the nineteenth century, is given. Long a ruin it was at first an important place from its position, and on one occasion the scene of a very violent contest between the Camerons and the Macleans. The operations connected with the formation of the Caledonian Canal brought about the entire destruction of the buildings, although a part of the castle and a portion of the surrounding moat remained in my own recollection. It was occupied by David Baillie, first of Dochfour, as late as 1671.

Surrounded with foes and situated at a great distance from their own chief and kin, in the County of Argyle,

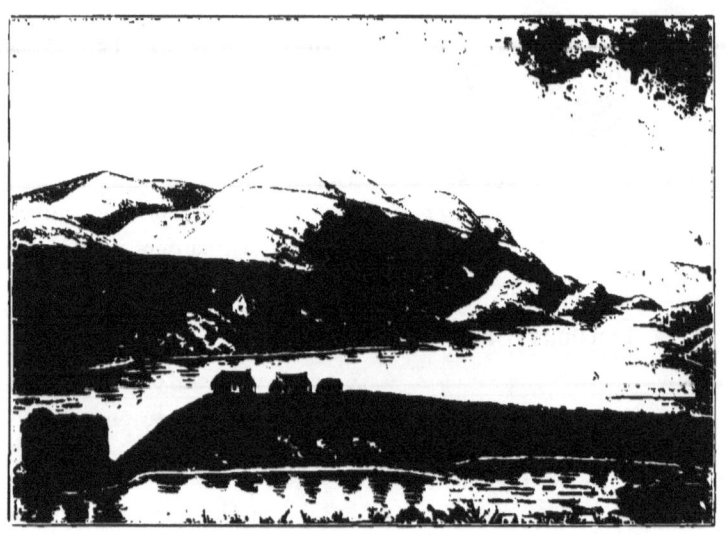

CASTLE SPIRIDAN, BONA FERRY, STRATHERRICK HILLS, AND LOCH NESS. FROM A SKETCH IN 1804.

the Northern Macleans for their own safety took protection of, and associated themselves with, the Clan Chattan, then a rising and absorbing Confederation. Sir Eneas Mackintosh places them as No. 9 of the associated tribes; and that they took protection about the year 1400. Kinrara in his history, dealing with the period of Malcolm, 10th Mackintosh, says that "Margaret his third daughter by his wife Mora, daughter of the Laird of Moidart, married Hector Mac Tearlach, Chief of the Clan Tearlach, and that thereafter he gave his bond of service and man rent to Mackintosh, for himself and his posterity."

II.— Hector Maclean, 2nd of Clan Tearlach, lived for some time at Urquhart, at the place now called Balmacaan, really Bal mac Eachin, or the seat of Hector. At a later period he lived at Castle Spiritan, where it is said he was killed. The position of the Macleans of the North, military settlers from a distance, was a critical one. The Lordship of Urquhart had fallen into the hands of the Crown, and prior to the ultimate and lasting acquisition by the Grants, was constantly plundered and over run by neighbouring potentates from the East and West.

It is said that the Macleans had a charter to the lands of Urquhart, and Barony of Bona, but I have not been able to verify the point, and the position of Hector and of his son Farquhar was precarious, ultimately resulting in their being dispossessed of Urquhart and Bona. Hector was succeeded by his son

III.—Farquhar Maclean. Little is known of the third Maclean, but it has been handed down that he was called Farquhar "Gorrach," or the silly, from allowing himself to be overreached by the new possessors of Urquhart. Members of his family, male and female, held high ecclesiastical positions in Iona and elsewhere, such as Agnes and Marion Maclean,

Prioresses of Iona, and one was Bishop of the Isles, owning according to Dean Munro, the estate of Raasay "by heritage," but significantly adding, "but by Mac Gillie Callum (Macleod of Raasay) by the sword." Farquhar's son,

IV.—Donald Maclean, was infeft in Raasay as well as his son Alexander Maclean, and the Macleans up to the year 1632, made repeated attempts to resume possession. The genealogy of the Macleans is distinctly given in the Precept of Clare Constat by John, Bishop of the Isles, perpetual commendator of the monastery of St. Columba in Iona, with consent of his Archdeacon and Canons, dated at Edinburgh, 10th January, 1631, in favour of Alexander Maclean, son of the late Donald Maclean, son of Farquhar, son of Hector, of the eight merks land of Raasay, and three merks in Trotternish. In 1557, Donald Maclean, described as "in Dochgarroch," is one of the Jurymen at Inverness in the service of Lachlan Mackinnon as heir to his father the deceased Ewen Mackinnon of Mackinnon. From and after 1557 to 1832, the Macleans possessed Dochgarroch, at first on redeemable rights; but latterly by charter from the Gordons, the Superiors, in 1623, confirmed by the Crown in 1635.

V.—Alexander, eldest son of Donald, succeeded prior to 1600 and was the most important of his race. He was known as Alasdair vic Coil vic Fherquhar, and so described, is a party to the Great Bond of Union among the Clan Chattan, so frequently referred to in these pages, dated 4th April, 1609. He was succeeded by his son,

VI.—John Maclean, who married Agnes Fraser of Struy. His tombstone is in the Grey Friars churchyard of Inverness, wherein he is described as "an honest man and worthy gentleman." He died in 1674.

VII.—His eldest son, Alexander, married, 28th November, 1659, Agnes Chisholm of Comar, and died in the month of September, 1671, having predeceased his father, although propelled into the property. The next Dochgarroch was Alexander's eldest son,

VIII.—John Maclean, who married, in 1682, Miss Margaret Fowler of Inverness, member of an important Ross-shire family. He fought at Killiecrankie, and exerted himself so greatly for King James as to embarrass his estate. John's third son, Donald, removed to Argyll, and his descendant, Lieutenant-Colonel Alexander Maclean, of the 3rd West India Regiment, has been the greatest benefactor to the name of Maclean, educationally and otherwise, of all others of the name. His large bequests are now carefully and beneficially administered by the Lord Provost and Magistrates of Glasgow.

IX.—John Maclean of Dochgarroch, eldest son of John 8th hereof, succeeded prior to 1710, and following the example of his father, took an active part for the Stuarts in 1715, and as one of the Captains in the regiment of Clan Chattan. He married Christina, eldest daughter of Alexander Dallas of Cantray, head of a family of long standing in the North, and was succeeded by his son,

X.—Charles Maclean, some time an officer in the Black Watch, who is found in possession in the year 1752. By his wife, Marjorie Mackintosh of Drummond, he had four sons and three daughters. He died in 1778, being succeeded by his eldest son,

XI.—John, a youth of good promise, who, seeking his fortune in the West Indies, at an early age, met with what was then called "a stroke of the sun," necessitating his being sent home, deprived of reason. In this unhappy state he lingered on until his death in 1826, when the second brother, Captain Phineas Maclean, having previously died in Calicut,

OLD HOUSE OF DOCHGARROCH.

in the East Indies, the succession opened to the third son of Charles, viz.,

XII.—William Maclean, a Captain in the British service, in whose time Dochgarroch had to be sold. He died in 1841, and a view of his abode is here given, which has long since disappeared. He was succeeded by his eldest son,

XIII.—Allan Maclean, formerly of the Naval Pay Office, Greenwich, afterwards one of the Magistrates of Inverness. He had two brothers, the elder, Charles, for nearly forty years an officer, and afterwards Lieutenant-Colonel of the 72nd Highlanders, and the younger, who ultimately became the representative.

XIV.—William Maclean of Dochgarroch, who resided most of his life in England, where he died. At his death he was succeeded by his eldest surviving son,

XV.—Allan Maclean, the present Dochgarroch, who is married, and has two sons and one daughter, the eldest son being the Rev. Allan Mackintosh Maclean, 16th in descent from Sir Charles Maclean, who first settled in the North.

The Macleans of the North were long members of the Clan Chattan, and I have included them, being, according to Sir Eneas Mackintosh's History, placed No. 9 of the associated tribes. Up to this day there are several Macleans, remains of the ancient family, in the parishes of Urquhart and Bona.

Through their dissociation to a great extent with the North for the last sixty years, the Dochgarroch Macleans have naturally drawn back to their original clan of Duart. The present Macleans are hearty supporters and chieftains of that flourishing body, the Clan Maclean Association, in Glasgow.

No. X—THE MACINTYRES OF BADENOCH.
Clann an t-Saoir.

Sir Eneas Mackintosh places Clan Inteir, otherwise Macintyres of Badenoch, No. 16 of the associated tribes, and says they took protection of William, afterwards 13th Mackintosh, anno. 1496.

The Kinrara Historian says, under the heading of the above William :—" It was this William in an expedition to Rannoch and Appin, took the bard Macintyre (of whom the Macintyres of Badenoch are descended) under his protection. It was he who composed the excellent Erse Epitaph in joint commendation of Farquhar vic Conchie, and William vic Lachlan Badenoch, 12th and 13th Lairds of Mackintosh." Some have thought that the ancient and famous pibroch, "Mackintosh's Lament" is that above referred to; but judging from the few words of the refrain, being all that is known as authentic of the original, I am inclined to attribute the lament as composed in memory of William 15th Mackintosh, murdered by order of the Earl of Huntly, at Strathbogie, in 1550.

The name Macintyre is understood to be derived from the occupation of the first, who was a Turner or Wright, in Gaelic, Saoir.

It is of the misfortunes attending anything old, either to be obscured, or altered to suit the designs of unprincipled persons. While it was almost pardonable in a Macdonald, to designate this famous lament as "The lament of

MACINTYRE.

the grandson of Arisaig," a district long and inseparably connected with the Macdonalds, yet the Reverend Collector had some justification for his clever adaptation, in saying what was true, but at same time misleading. The Mackintoshes of old, had some time, through marriage, the designation of "Mac-mhic-a-Arasaig," though in the Rev. Peter Macdonald's time, it had for centuries been in abeyance. Once more I take the opportunity of protesting against the truly absurd words which of late have been put in circulation to the pibroch of "Mackintosh's Lament," in remembrance of a mythical Hugh Mackintosh, a name not to be found among the twenty-seven predecessors of The Mackintosh.

The descendants of the bard Macintyre settled in Badenoch, and were, like the MacVurrichs in the case of Clan Ranald—Maccrimmons in the case of Macleod—Macarthurs in the case of the Macdonalds of Sleat—hereditary bards to the Mackintoshes, and the Clan Chattan. As they possessed no land as owners, their history as a distinct sept is obscure, and at the present day there are but few living in Badenoch. Mr. S. F. Mackintosh of Farr, in his Collections (1832) thus refers to the Macintyres, "No. 16. The Clan Intier. This was a branch of the Macintyres of Gleno, who formerly possessed the sides of Loch Laggan in Badenoch; many families of whom are still in that quarter." In the last century one of the clan, Lieutenant-General John Macintyre, born at Knappach, in the parish of Kingussie, was a distinguished soldier in the service of the East India Company. The grandfather of one of the sept, whom I had the pleasure of knowing in Parliament, the late Mr. E. J.

S

Macintyre, Q.C., was a native of the parish of Moy, and my late friend often told me he was much attached to the place where his predecessors lived, and that he was proud of being of Clan Chattan.

In Celtic poetry and literature, the names of Duncan Bàn Macintyre, the Rev. Dr. Macintyre of Kilmonivaig, whose father was some time minister of Laggan, and the Reverend Donald Macintyre of Kincardine, will readily occur amongst those conferring lustre on the name.

The name of Miss Margaret Macintyre, the famous *prima donna* of the North, deserves honourable recognition.

The name is presently numerous and influential, and all who are of the Badenoch Macintyres should fix upon a head, and re-uniting themselves, take up their proper position in the Clan.

No. XI.—THE CLAN TARRILL.

THIS ancient sept has distinctively long disappeared, having become incorporated with the name of Mackintosh.

Being undoubtedly of Clan Chattan, and placed as No. 6 of the associated tribes of Clan Chattan by Sir Eneas Mackintosh—in any history of the clan, they can not, and should not be either overlooked or omitted, particularly when it is considered that their virtual extirpation occurred in a clan battle. Sir Eneas Mackintosh, in placing them as No. 6 says, that they took protection of William, 7th of Mackintosh, in 1350.

Kinrara, in his history, referring to the period of Lachlan, 8th Mackintosh, says, that in this Lachlan's time "the Clan Tarrill, a family that lived in Petty, and were constant followers of the Lairds of Mackintosh, were in a flourishing condition." The death of the above Lachlan Mackintosh is recorded as having occurred 4th November, 1407.

The late Mr. S. F. Mackintosh of Farr, in his Collections made over fifty years ago, referring to the associated tribes, enumerates as "No. 6 the Clan Tarrill from Ross-shire. Of this tribe there are now several in Strathnairn who call themselves Mackintoshes." Following up this indication that the sept came originally from the County of Ross, it is found in the Calder papers, published by the old Spalding Club, that in the year 1457 the names of Andrew Tarrill, and of his deceased wife Janet, are among the Crown vassals within the Earldom of Ross, and included in the Collecting

Book of the Chamberlain, William of Calder. The lands appear to be those of Killen and Pitfour, Parish of Avoch, and as there are to the present day important lands called Meikle and Little Tarrell in said county, the origin of the family as from Ross seems clear. In the year 1449 Thomas Tarrill appears to be proprietor of the estate of Skibo.

The last time Clan Tarrill is found in the field as a distinctive tribe occurred a few years before the death of Malcolm, 10th Mackintosh, who died about 1457. The event is recorded under the head of Duncan Mackintosh, 11th Mackintosh, as he, during the last years of his father's life in extreme old age, took the leading part. The circumstances are thus recorded by Kinrara:—

"Duncan Mackintosh, Captain of Clan Chattan, was a man of a meek and quiet disposition, and not subject to much trouble in his time, for his father had so composed and ordered his affairs in Lochaber, and daunted his enemies there and elsewhere, that the son was not much troubled or disquieted on that account after his father's death. He is not recorded to have the chief leading of the Clan Chattan at any memorable fight while his father lived, save once. This arose from a sudden recontre, which he and his two brethren, Lachlan and Allan (Lachlan Badenoch and Allan, first of Kellachie), with a few of their friends had against Giliespic Macdonald (according to other historians, Celestine Macdonald), natural brother of the Earl of Ross, at the recovery of a spreath of cattle which the said Gillespic and his associates had taken out of Petty. Both parties met at Culloden, when after a bloody fight, Gillespic and his accomplices, (howbeit by far the greater number) were routed, the spreath recovered, and the greater part of the drivers killed. Yet not without great loss to Mackintosh, for a branch of the Clan Chattan, called Clan Tarrill, were that day almost extirpated. This fell out some years before the death of Malcolm, Laird of Mackintosh, who at that time was a very old man.'

From and after the fight, which occurred probably about 1450, Clan Tarrill as a sept sunk, although in 1672, the Lord Lyon enumerates them as of Clan Chattan, and the descendants of the few survivors in course of time called themselves Mackintoshes. The Tarralaichs had their burial place in Dalarossie; the grounds can still be identified. Of this race is Mr. Lachlan Mackintosh, Postmaster of Daviot, who with others gladly count themselves as of Clan Tarrill.

The etymology of the name Tarrill has been explained to me by that accomplished Celtic scholar, Mr. Alexander MacBain, Rector of the High School of Inverness, as in Gaelic "Tarralaich," in English "Harald," and that the designation "na Tarralaich" is occasionally used by old people at the present day in Strathnairn and Strathdearn.

As the Clan Tarrill had their chief abode in Petty, with this light thrown on the name by Mr. MacBain, there is no difficulty in identifying as one of them, "John Makherald roy," a sufferer in the hership of Petty by the Dunbars, in 1502; or in another at a much earlier date, being a man of standing, "Augusius Haraldi," one of the Inquest in the succession to the lands of Geddes.

No. XII.—THE MACANDREWS.
Sliochd Gill' Andris.

This Sept is placed by Sir Eneas Mackintosh as No. 11 of Clan Chattan, and adds, "that they took protection of Mackintosh about 1400." The Kinrara historian, under the head of Malcolm, tenth Mackintosh, after recording the association of the Macqueens or clan Revan, goes on to say— "And sicklike Donald MacGillandrish, of whom the Clan Andrish are named, came out of Muidart, with Mora Macdonald, Lady Mackintosh."

It is thus seen that the Macqueens and Macandrews of Clan Chattan, originally and at the same time, came from Muidart, in the train of the bride Mora Macdonald, daughter of Clan Ranald. The descendants of the above Donald Mac Gillandrish, settled in Connage of Petty, at the time a favourite abode of the Mackintoshes, and in course of time the name was anglicized into Macandrew, or found to be so by scribes, as more euphonious. The name of Gillanders is in the same way a variation of the original Gaelic.

After the hership of the Lordship of Petty and of the Ogilvies, these eastern invaders took steps to recover their losses sustained by and through the Clan Chattan, the old possessors, and in the year 1516-17, the name of William Mac Gillandrish is found amongst those summoned for the spuilzie.

Possessing no lands, the after history of the Macandrews of Clan Chattan, is obscure; but the name of that notable

Bowman, John beg MacAndrew of Delnahatnich, who flourished in the middle of the 17th century, may be included among the celebrities of the name.

In the present century, the name has come well to the front. Donald Macandrew, who resided near the Bridge of Dulsie, was progenitor of a race, who for three generations have been prominent in the north. His son George, Land Surveyor, held important offices in the Counties of Inverness and Nairn. He was succeeded by his son, John, the well-known, talented Solicitor of Inverness; and he in turn by his son the present Sir Henry Cockburn Macandrew, alike prominent in law, soldiering, literature, and politics. The progress of this family has been steadily upward, and its members have been and truly are a credit to the North and to Clan Chattan. The name of the late Sir W. P. Andrew, a native of Inverness, so long prominent in Eastern affairs and the opening up of traffic routes to the East, should not be forgotten.

Nos. XIII., XIV., XV., AND XVI.

As we have now arrived towards the end of the sixteen associated tribes of Clan Chattan, it may be as well to give the complete list as written down by Sir Eneas Mackintosh upwards of a century since. These run as follows:—

MINOR SEPTS OF CLAN CHATTAN.

1.—The Clan vic Gillivray, 1271.
2.—The Clan Wurrich (Macphersons), 1291.
3.—The Clan Vean (Macbeans), 1292.
4.—The Clan Day (Davidsons), 1350.
5.—The Clan vic Gories, 1369.
6.—The Clan Tarrall, 1372.
7.—The Clan Chean duy, Glen Beg of Strathnairn, 1373.
8.—The Sliochd Gow Chruim (Gows), 1399.
9.—The Clan Tearlich (Macleans of the North), 1400.
10.—The Clan Revan (Macqueens), 1400.
11.—The Clan vic Gillandrish Connage (Macandrews), 1400.
12.—The Clan Clerichs (Clarks), 1400.
13.—The Sliochd Gillie Vor Mac Aonas, 1485.
14.—The Clan Phail (Macphails), 1500.
15.—The Clan Finlay Cheir, 1502.
16.—The Clan Inteir (Macintyres), 1496.

I have abstained from referring to No. 2 of the above list, as judging by their ancestors, their dignity might be hurt, if placed under the heading of this book. Want of authentic material and the decay of the septs, has compelled four in the above list, viz: Nos. 5, 7, 13, and 15, to be put in one chapter.

No. XIII.—VIC GORIES.

This sept is placed by Sir Eneas Mackintosh as No. 5, who says they took protection of Lachlan, 8th Mackintosh, anno 1369. No reference to the sept is made by the Kinrara historian, and I am disposed to think that this word should be Gorrie, or Godfred, as a few years after the above date the name of Donald Gorrie Mackintosh is mentioned.

No. XIV.—THE CLAN DHU OF STRATHNAIRN.

THIS clan is placed No. 7 by Sir Eneas Mackintosh, under the head of "The Clan Dhu, Glenbeg of Strathnairn," who adds, they took protection of Lachlan, 8th Mackintosh, anno 1373. The Kinrara historian, under the head of the above Lachlan, narrates, "In his time lived Gillie Phadrig vic Iain, commonly called Iain Dhu vic Iain," the progenitor of the Clan Dhu.

No. XV.—THE SLIOCHD GILLIE VOR MAC AONAS.

SIR ENEAS MACKINTOSH places this sept as No. 13 of Clan Chattan, and states that they took protection of Duncan, 11th Mackintosh, anno 1485. The Kinrara historian, under the head of the above Duncan, says, "In his time Angus, the father of Mulmore, of whom the Sliochd Gillie-mor-vic-Aonas are so called, had their beginning."

No. XVI.—THE CLAN FINLAY CHEIR.

This sept is placed by Sir Eneas Mackintosh as No. 15 of the associated tribes, and says that they took protection of Farquhar, 12th Mackintosh, anno 1502, while the Kinrara historian says that they, with the Mac Aonas tribe above mentioned, and the Macphails, had their beginning in the time of the 12th Mackintosh.

If there be representatives of any of these four tribes, now that attention has been drawn to the matter, it is hoped they will come forward and assert their position.

The Farquharsons, like the Shaws, having been originally Mackintoshes, will next be dealt with, in so far as connected with Clan Chattan.

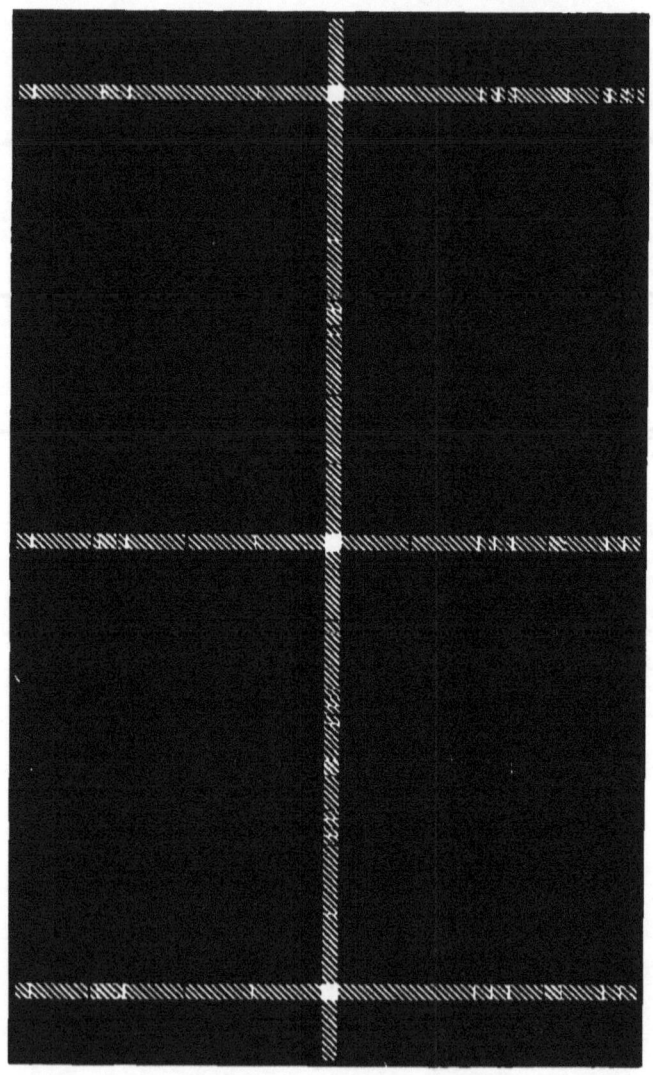

FARQUHARSON.

No. XVII.—THE FARQUHARSONS.

Clan Fionlay. Part First.

The Farquharsons, like the Shaws (No. 5 hereof), are placed by Sir Eneas Mackintosh as number 3 of the Clan Chattan descended of Mackintosh, his house.

They branched off from Alexander Ciar, the third Shaw of Rothiemurchus, who had married one of the Stuarts of Kincardine, their progenitor being Farquhar, the 4th son. Removing to Aberdeenshire, the descendants of this Farquhar were called Farquharson, and have long held a very influential position in North East Scotland. In their early history, the name of Farquhar's descendant, Finlay Mòr, Standard-bearer at Pinkie, where he fell, 1547, stands prominent, and from and after him the Farquharsons were called in Gaelic Clan Fionlay; of him also descended the surname of Mac Keracher.

By marriage with the heiress of MacHardy of Invercauld the Farquharsons acquired, as commonly reported, a large estate, and were much favoured with the family of Mar, of whom they held their lands. Holding for a long time an independent status, it is not here intended to do more than indicate their descent, their connection with Clan Chattan, and acknowledged dependence on its head. The present family of Invercauld is descended of the latter Rosses of Balnagown, formerly

Lockharts, and as it is publicly announced that selections from their valuable papers are in course of publication, there is no occasion at present to enter into full details. It is to

From R. Ronald M'Ian's] FARQUHARSON. [*"Clans of the Scottish Highlands.*

be hoped, in the cause of truth, that there will be no repetition of the inaccuracies and falsehoods of that Farquharson historian who flourished over 200 years since, repeated in

Burke (Edition 1894) asserting that the Farquharsons are direct descendants of the Earls of Fife, without referring to the Mackintoshes and Shaws as intervening.

The first time I have observed the Farquharsons formally acknowledging Mackintosh as their chief, in writing, was upon 31st March, 1595. At Invercauld, upon that day, five influential Farquharsons, together with Mackintosh of Dalmunzie, in Strathardle, and MacOmie of Glenshee, both in Perthshire, enter into the obligation after quoted, and it will not be overlooked, that Invercauld's name is not the first, nor placed in the leading position. In truth, Donald was the elder brother.

"At Endercauld this last day of March in the year of God 1595; It is appointed and agreed upon betwixt honourable and discreet persons, they are to say, Lachlan Mackintosh of Dunachton on the one part; and James Mackintosh of Gask, Donald Farquharson of Tulligermont, John Farquharson of Invercauld, George, Lachlan, and Finlay Farquharson, brothers to the said Donald, on the other part,—in manner subsequent.— That is to say the said Lachlan Mackintosh having touched the Holy Evangell by the tenor hereof upon his great oath, faithfully promises to fortify, maintain, and assist and defend the said James Mackintosh, Donald, John, George, Lachlan and Finlay Farquharsons, their sons and friends, to the uttermost of his power, as also their heirs, in all their adoes, directly and indirectly against all whatsomever persons within this Realm (the King's Majesty being excepted); and likewise that he shall never enterprize or attempt any great matter of weight or consequence, whereby he or his said friends may come or fall in deadly feud, without the advice of the foresaid persons had thereto; and gif he does in the contrary, they shall not be holden to assist or maintain him thereunto, notwithstanding of their faithful promise after specified, but they to be free thereof as if the same had never been made. For the whilk causes and upon the provision aforesaid the said James Mackintosh of Gask, Donald, John, George, Lachlan, and Finlay Farquharson,—and with them Duncan

Mackintosh of Dalmunzie, and Robert MacHomie in the Burn of Glenshee, having touched the Holy Evangells, by the tenor hereof, and upon their great oaths, faithfully promise and oblige them and their heirs, to maintain, fortify, serve and defend the said Lachlan Mackintosh, his heirs, as our natural Chief, at our utmost power in all his adoes directly or indirectly against all and whatsoever person or persons within this Realm (The King's Majesty being excepted) and the premises observed. In witness whereof baith the said parties respectively subscribing (that can write) and the rest given their oaths upon the present Bond, day and date foresaid before these Witnesses, Sir Thomas Gordon of Cluny and diverse others."

Although numerous and influential, with Invercauld in course of time as undoubted head, yet it is found that as late as 1618, Invercauld is not included amongst the Chiefs called upon by Act of Parliament to answer for their clans.

In 1634 Robert Farquharson of Invercauld, and James Farquharson, W. S., are the Judges and Arbitrators named by William Mackintosh of that ilk, while arranging the serious question with Grant, his late guardian, and the large sums claimed as owing to the minor's estate. In 1643, the said William Mackintosh procures Robert Farquharson of Invercauld and William Mackintosh of Kelachie as cautioners for a pressing debt, and grants them security over his Lochaber Estates. Robert's son, Alexander, married Isabella Mackintosh, daughter of the above mentioned William Mackintosh. Their second, and surviving son, John Farquharson, and Lachlan Mackintosh of Mackintosh, who distinguished themselves in the '15, as aftermentioned, were thus cousins in the first and second degree.

In 1664, Lachlan Mackintosh, 19th Mackintosh, resolved to bring the 300 years' quarrel with the Camerons to a final issue, and summoned all his friends, vassals and kin. In the List of Deeds will be found *fac simile* of the very important deed granted by the Clan. It is in the hand-writing of Lachlan Mackintosh of Kinrara, the historian, whom I have so frequently quoted, and is titled "Bond be certane of the name

INVERCAULD HOUSE.

of Clan Chattan, to their Chieff, dated 19th Nov. 1664," and is signed by 6 Macphersons, 5 Mackintoshes, 4 Farquharsons, 3 MacGillivrays, 2 Macbeans, 2 Shaws, 1 Macqueen, with two by initials, all men of position and standing. The Farquharsons who subscribed were—1. James Farquharson of Inverey. 2. Charles Farquharson of Monaltrie. 3. James Farquharson, younger of Whitehouse, who died s. p.; and 4. George Farquharson, without designation, probably Bronchdearg.

Thwarted by powerful ill-wishers and determined foes, amongst others by the Marquis of Huntly, the Earls of Aboyne and of Moray in the North and East, the Earls of Argyle and Breadalbane in the West and South, who created dissensions among the Clan Chattan, Mackintosh had for a time to forbear.

In the rising of 1715, John Farquharson of Invercauld, with 4 officers and 140 men, joined the Clan Chattan regiment, in which he was Lieutenant-Colonel, and accompanying it to England, was taken prisoner at Preston.

Farquharson of Inverey, Invercauld's near relative, took it upon him to raise some of the Farquharsons as a distinct body in Lord Mar's army.

Writing of the episode of 1715, Mrs. Anne Duff, the old Lady Mackintosh, in her memoir says, "The Earl of Mar was some time at Braemar, in his vassal, Invercauld's house, who stood out some time, and a great many more thoughtful people." Referring to the affair of Preston, Lady Mackintosh says, "Mackintosh and Invercauld having the most dangerous post, behaved most manfully, with a great character from strangers as acting their part with victory and courage." Detailing her husband's capture and imprisonment, she gives the highest credit to Sir David Dalrymple, King's Advocate, for his intercession, which in the end resulted in Mackintosh and Invercauld's liberation without trial. Lady Mackintosh says, "they were both released the same day (9th August, 1716), having been in prison for about ten months."

In 1724 Invercauld and Inverey are parties to the Deed of Renunciation by Cluny to Mackintosh, as are their representatives, John of Invercauld and Alexander of Inverey, to the deed of 1756, before referred to. In an agreement dated Moy Hall, 20th September, 1732, twixt Mackintosh and the Dowager Lady Mackintosh, John Farquharson of Invercauld and Francis Farquharson, second lawful son to Alexander Farquharson of Monaltrie, are witnesses.

In the year 1741 Anne Farquharson, daughter of Invercauld before referred to, by one of the Athole family, married Eneas, 22nd Mackintosh, and during the rising of 1745, she took such a leading part for the Stuarts as to be called "Colonel Anne." It says much for the prudence and discretion of this most honoured lady, who shares with Eva nic Gille Chattan, the deepest affection of the Clan Chattan, that in her husband's disqualification from holding a command in the old 42nd, she did not select as temporary leader from many well qualified members of her own family, but fixed on the gallant Alexander MacGillivray of Dunmaglass. Her portrait, taken from the original at Moy Hall, is given on next page.

At Culloden the Farquharsons mustered over 300 men. John Farquharson, remembering his pardon in 1716, and arrived at mature age—for I find a note regarding him in 1686—did not go out, nor permit his son, although Jacobite feeling strongly prevailed among the clan. Upon the death of James Farquharson, son and successor of John, without male issue, the old close continuous friendship and alliance with the Mackintoshes ceased. It might have been well for Clan Chattan had the views of certain sagacious looking-ahead friends

to bring about, in a certain way, a permanent alliance at Culloden been listened to by the principals. The Clan Chattan were placed 5th in the right division and the Farquharsons 4th in the left, in other words both well to the centre of the front line, near each other.

In the trial of Captain John Farquharson, a witness deponed that "John was Captain in Colonel Farquharson's regiment, and in the march to Nairn to surprise the English the night before Culloden." Another witness deponed that "John Farquharson was at the head of the Farquharson regiment upon the field of battle at Culloden when preparing to attack the Hanoverian forces."

Francis Farquharson of Monaltrie, nephew of Invercauld, commanded the Farquharsons. Some days before the battle of Culloden, a witness at his trial said he saw him some days before, with a big blue coat on, at the head of his own regiment, which was then drawn out with Ardsheil's regiment and some of the Macleods, upon a plain about a mile from Inverness (The Wester Haugh—C. F. M.), and that they went through their exercises, and were reviewed by the Pretender's (sic) son. Another witness describes Colonel Farquharson as "a tall man with thin face, dressed in Highland garb, with sword and pistols and white cockade." The Colonel's servant, John Reach, who had been with his master thirty years, said "his master joined at Edinburgh with 30 men, and went back to raise more." Colonel Farquharson was condemned but reprieved.

The name of Balmoral is now often heard of since its acquisition by Her Majesty, who has made Braemar her favourite residence. Let us look at the owner in 1745. James Farquharson of Balmoral's accession and acts in the '45 are described by himself, when brought to trial long after the battle of Culloden. In a Memorial to the Crown dated 21st November, 1748, he says, putting all the blame on his brother:—

"That in the month of October, 1745, your petitioner, who till then lived quiet and peaceable at his own house in the County of Aberdeen, was unhappily induced to join in the late Rebellion, at the instigation of an elder brother, whom he still regarded as a parent.

That your petitioner is informed upon this account, he is excepted from your Majesty's Gracious Act of Indemnity, and that an indictment has been lately found against him before a grand jury at Edinburgh for high treason.

That your petitioner begs leave with the greatest humility to represent to your Majesty that from the time of his appearing in arms in the latter end of October, 1745, it was his constant care to the utmost of his power to prevent distresses to your Majesty's faithful subjects, and to protect them from injury in their persons and estates, and particularly those who had the misfortune to fall into the hands of the rebels as many of them can, and the petitioner believes will, testify when called upon.

That in the beginning of February thereafter, your petitioner retired 'home again' to his own country, and has ever since lived in such a manner as not to give the smallest offence.

That your petitioner is now advanced to a considerable age, and his health impaired by the many hardships and distresses which he had suffered.

That your petitioner has presumed in these circumstances, not as an alleviation of his guilt, but in order to move your Majesty's compassion, and being heartily sorry for his offence, he most most humbly submits himself to your Majesty's Royal clemency, and imploring your Royal mercy, promises for the future to live a grateful and dutiful subject.

And your petitioner shall ever pray,
(Signed) JAMES FARQUHARSON.

In support of his prayer, the Moderator and the Ministers of the Presbytery of Alford transmitted a strongly worded statement testifying to his character. It is signed by the following:—

Pat Thomas, Minister at Tough, Modr.
Pat Reid, Clatt.
Theodore Gordon, Kinnethmont.

James Lumsden, Strathdon.
John Maxwell, Auchindown.
Walter Syme, Tillienish?
Alexander Strachan, Keig.
Thomas Reid, Leochel.
Alexander Johnston, Alford.
Alexander Drew, Forbes,
William Milne, Kildrummie.

The Moderator and Ministers of Kincardine O'Neal petition in similar terms :—

George Campbell, Moderator.
W. Mackenzie, Glenmuick.
Alexander Garden, Birse.
Francis Dauncey, Lumphanan.
William Abel, Kincardine O'Neal.
Alexander Garrioch, Midmar.
Robert Michie, Cluny.
John MacInnes, Colstrew.
James Paterson, Coull.
George Shepherd, Tarland.
George Shepherd, Aboyne.

Mr. Charles Maitland, Advocate, Principal John Chalmers, Aberdeen, and James Paterson, Sheriff Depute of Stirlingshire, also bear testimony that they have been prisoners, and met with great civility, attention, and kindness from Balmoral. He was found guilty and ultimately discharged.

The extracts from the State Papers were supplied to me by Mr. D. Murray Rose, who is exceedingly well posted up in all that took place in 1745.

In 1737 James Farquharson of Invercauld executed a deed of entail of his extensive estates in Braemar and Strath Dee, and calls to the succession his only son, James, his brother, Alexander Farquharson of Monaltrie, and his four daughters, Ann, afterwards Lady Mackintosh, Margaret, Frances, and Jean. By the deed it would appear that Invercauld proper extended to $1\frac{1}{2}$ davoch of land, Castleton of Braemar 1 davoch, Monaltrie 1 davoch, Crathie $\frac{1}{2}$ davoch, Brackley in Glengairn $1\frac{1}{2}$ davoch, and there are numerous other places mentioned in the entail. James Farquharson died in 1750, and was described "as a man of great honour and merit." He was succeeded by his son, also named James, who appears to have been in 1745 a Captain of Foot in the Hanoverian army; he died in 1806, after being in possession of the estates for fifty-six years. In 1756 he signs the deed in favour of his brother-in-law, Mackintosh, recovering the Loch Laggan lands. The Farquharsons were all vassals of Mar, and on the downfall of that family did not take kindly to the new owners, descendants of Muldavit and of the meal dealing Braco. The new family not only asserted its rights but strove to enlarge its holding in Braemar. This after many years was accomplished in the year 1784, as far as regarded the important estate of Invercy, which, formerly Invercy and Innerie, has been changed by the present owners to Inveraye. Rose of Montcoffer, the active and indefatigable doer for the Muldavit family, which had broken out into the Lordship of Braco and Earldom of Fife, in that refuge for ambitious plutocratic commoners—the Peerage of Ireland —thus narrates his doings in the autumn of 1784:—

"It was now time to strike in with Haughton for the purchase of Inverey and Auchindrane, as to which my instructions were unlimited. Met with Haughton, and after a great deal of trouble concluded a bargain for the estates at 34 years' purchase."

In the end of September, 1784, Montcoffer visited the new purchase and records :—

"Inspected the bounds of Inverey with James Stewart. Went to Gleny, Cairn-a-Grinish, Dalnaglac, dividing Gleny from Glen Cluny, Craignish, Altalet, and above that Hell's Glen. Travelled with James Stewart over Delrudalet and Amuchnamon, and reported the extent, and formed rules and regulations for pasturages, sheilings, forests, and game."

Lord Braco had purchased the vast estate of the Earls of Mar, after that family had sunk in the troubles of 1715, but, as before mentioned, was not welcomed by the neighbours, mostly vassals of Mar, under which family they had been nourished, and greatly flourished.

Some years previous to the above purchase, a combination of the chief proprietors of the Braemar Highlands had been formed against the Duffs, and in especial in regard to woods. This combination was headed by Invercauld, and supported by the Earl of Aboyne, the Farquharsons of Rynallan, Monaltrie, Crathinard, Inverey, and others. This powerful combination was met by Montcoffer, who complacently records under date 1780, after the contest had been running on for years, that :—

"At Mar Lodge he attempted a compromise with Invercauld, Inverei, and Monaltrie, and proceeding to the Marlie, where Invercauld dwelt, failed with him, but going on to Balmoral settled with Inverie, and by the after withdrawal of Lord Aboyne, Abergeldie, and Crathinard, demolished the combination."

The Fife troubles did not cease, however, for next year, 1781. Montcoffer says :—

"Monaltrie at this time had done a very bare faced act, cut *brevi manu* the stately firs in sight of Mar Lodge. Some evil person set fire to the woods of Badness and Beachan. Alexander Lamond, James MacGregor, James Small, and others, cut woods at their own hand, poinded cattle in Garrieduran, within the forest of Guilzie, and Invercauld's people or herds set fire to the skirts of the woods of Caich and Ballochbuie, and erected sheilings hard by."

It may be added that poor Montcoffer, who managed with extraordinary success all the Fife affairs, territorially and politically, on a miserable salary, after a service extending over thirty years, and having put many tangled matters to rights, consolidated and enlarged the estates, was dismissed, and had to pursue his late employer in the law courts for redress.

James Farquharson of Invercauld, at his death in 1806, left no male issue, and was succeeded under the destination of the entail by his only surviving child, Catharine. Well wishers of the Clan Chattan had, even before marriageable age, suggested a suitable matrimonial alliance for this great heiress, but it came to naught, and the person selected was one of that lucky Lockhart family, who in a previous generation had obtained possession of the great estate of Balnagown in the Counties of Ross and Sutherland. The present owner of Invercauld is Catharine Farquharson's great grandson. As may be seen from the illustration on page 151, the house is a noble residence.

In dealing with branches of the Farquharsons, I shall

confine myself to those more closely connected with the Clan Chattan, parties to the Bond of 1664.

I.—INVERIE.—This family descended of James, 4th son of Donald of Castleton, and were prominent in the clan. In the time of William of Inverie, second of the family, occurred a serious quarrel with the Gordons. It is thus narrated by Mackintosh of Kinrara in his Latin history, and as it took place in his own day, and came under his personal cognizance, may be taken as strictly authentic:—

"In the month of September, 1666, there fell out some slaughter betwixt certain of the name of Gordon and the Farquharsons of Braemar, which bred the Laird of Mackintosh some trouble, and had engaged these two families in a far greater, if the business had not been prudently managed, and the evil for the time prevented. The matter fell out thus:

John Gordon of Breacklie having commission from the Town Council of Aberdeen for fining such as killed black fish on the water of Dee, did outlaw some of the name of Farquharson and their tenants in a most rigid manner; and upon the 15th day of September foresaid, having convened a number of his tenants and followers, did beset certain Braemar men on the highway as they were coming from a fair that held at Kilmuir in Angus, and having beaten some of them, did in a very illegal manner take from them 16 to 18 pairs of horses for a poind. On the 17th day of the foresaid month John Farquharson, apparent of Inverey (so well known as the "Black Colonel"—C.F.M.), the master of the most part of those who were robbed as aforesaid, being accompanied with the owners of the horses and others of his friends, came down to guard a fair that stands nearly at Tulloch (a mile he east the house of Breacklie), and on their way sent a message to Breacklie, desiring that in regard the foresaid poinding was unlawful, and that some of the horses poinded belonged to persons who were never outlawed for black fish, therefore he would be pleased to restore the horses to the owners, and he would engage himself that such persons as were guilty would do duty before their return from

V

Tulloch fair. Breacklie refused on any terms to restore the horses. Inverey was willing to dispense with the horses at that time, provided Breacklie would condescend to submit differences to well willed persons who would decide within four days after the foresaid market. As Breacklie was about to answer this overture, he perceived Alexander Gordon of Abergeldie with a number of armed men coming to his assistance, whereupon he disdained to parley any further upon the business, and in great passion and fury did pursue and assault Inverie and his tenants, with guns, pistols, and drawn swords. Inverie being most unwilling to enter in blood with his neighbours, at first gave ground, earnestly entreating Breacklie to desist from his pursuit, but Breacklie, Abergeldie, and his followers became the more insolent and eager, and in time shot two of Inverey's followers dead upon the spot. Whereupon Inverey and his tenants being forced in their own defence to resist the pursuers, faced about and killed the said John Gordon of Breacklie, William Gordon, his brother, and James Gordon of Cults, who were most forward in the pursuit. Shortly after this slaughter Breackle's nearest relations pursued Inverey and the most part of the specials of his friends, criminally before the justices. Then Inverey makes his address to Mackintosh as his chief, who remembering the kindness he had received of Inverey not long before in the expedition to Lochaber, did set his course to act a friendly part for him: and to manifest his forwardness and resolution to that effect, did travel from his own house to Edinburgh three several times in his defence. And by his friendship and moyen brought the business to that point that in the end there was no pursuer to appear in the cause, and in a short time a deserving clansman had occasion to meet with a thankful requital from a loving chief."

The manner Inverie fell to the Duffs has already been mentioned, with Montcoffer's complaisant remarks on his success.

II.—MONALTRIE.—This estate, which has fallen into that of Invercauld, lies chiefly within the parish of Glenmuick and Glengairn. Charles Farquharson, last of the old family, sold the estate to Alexander, younger brother of Invercauld, in 1702, having been all his life the constant ally, friend and supporter of Mackintosh.

III.—WHITEHOUSE.—This family descends from James,  younger brother of Colonel Donald Farquharson (Donald Og), a distinguished soldier in the Civil Wars. The eldest son of the above James signs the Bond of 1664 as "younger of Whitehouse," and dying without issue, was succeeded by his brother, Henry. One of the family, Captain Henry Farquharson (whose portrait is given), fell at Culloden, a handsome gallant youth, one of the many of the flower of Highland families who fought and died for Prince Charlie. The portrait of his son and successor, Dr. William Farquharson, is given, and the line continued direct until 1896, when it terminated on the death, without

CAPTAIN HENRY FARQUHARSON,
WHO FELL AT CULLODEN.

DR. WILLIAM FARQUHARSON.

issue, of Andrew Farquharson. Mr. Farquharson had been a member of the Bombay House founded by Sir Charles Forbes, and on his retirement in 1840, received a very complimentary

PATRICK FARQUHARSON.

address from upwards of three hundred of the most influential Parsee merchants of Bombay. By his settlements the estate of Whitehouse was left to his great nephew, George

Leslie, younger son of Kininvie, on condition of assuming the name of Farquharson. This has been done, and the present Whitehouse (whose coat of arms is given) may be confidently

MARJORY STEWART, WIFE OF PATRICK FARQUHARSON.

expected to prove a credit to the name of Farquharson. The mansion house, erected by the late Andrew Farquharson, is reproduced, as also portraits of his parents, Patrick

ANDREW FARQUHARSON,
AT THE AGE OF 19.

Farquharson and Marjory Stewart, Lessmurdie, the latter of great character, also of himself when a youth of nineteen. Andrew Farquharson lived to the great age of ninety-three. Dying in 1896, without issue, the headship of the Farquharsons, which had been in Whitehouse for about a century, fell to Farquharson of Finzean, as after mentioned.

WHITEHOUSE, ABERDEENSHIRE.

IV.—HAUGHTON. This estate, which came by marriage to a member of the Altyre family, has after a brilliant course again descended in the female line, and now belongs to Miss Maria Ogilvie Farquharson. Her step-mother, Mrs. Farquharson of Haughton, takes much interest in Highland

R. F. O. FARQUHARSON.

MRS. FARQUHARSON.

matters, and in her clan. Mrs. Farquharson is a great authority on Ferns, and prior to her marriage, when Miss Marian Sarah Ridley, of Hollington, Hants, published " A Pocket Guide to British Ferns, London, 1881."

The late Mr. Robert Francis Ogilvie Farquharson, of Haughton, who had succeeded also to the estate of Thornton, died in 1890, much regretted. At a public meeting of the inhabitants of the Parish of Alford, where the deceased after returning from Australia, resided as the leading man of the

HAUGHTON HOUSE.

Parish for thirty-six years, a most gratifying tribute was passed to his memory, eulogizing him as a kind landlord, high agriculturist and prize winner, as also an active and useful man of business. A handsome fountain erected to his memory, adorns the village of Alford.

MINOR SEPTS OF CLAN CHATTAN.   169

V.—ALLARGUE AND BREDA.—General Farquharson, whose portrait is given, has had a famous career in India, reaching his present position after surmounting obstacles and crushing

MAJOR-GENERAL GEO. MACBAIN FARQUHARSON.

oppression in high quarters in a manner worthy of a Highlander and a Farquharson. Breda stands near the succession to the headship.

W

BREDA HOUSE.

VI.—FINZEAN.—I have left this family to the last, because, so far as has been observed, there seems no doubt that Dr. Robert Farquharson, who has, and is serving one of the divisions of his County in Parliament so faithfully, is the worthy Chief. Dr. Farquharson is directly descended of Robert, son of Donald Farquharson, otherwise Mackintosh, 2nd of Castleton of Braemar. Robert married Margaret, daughter of Lachlan Mor Mackintosh of Mackintosh and widow of Glengarry. Since the death of Andrew Farquharson of Whitehouse in 1896, unmarried, Dr. Farquharson has become head of all the Farquharsons. To his very advanced political opinions he has always adhered. Dr. Farquharson is well qualified to represent the best traditions of the celebrated house of Farquhar Mor. Illustrations of the picturesque house of Finzean, and of Dr. Farquharson at home, surrounded by friends, are given.

I have to express my acknowledgments to the four families

DR. FARQUHARSON AND FRIENDS.

immediately above mentioned for their courtesy in responding to enquiries and requests, and allowing so many rare and valued illustrations to appear; and to express my regret that the scope of the work does not permit of my doing them the full justice their position demands.

FINZEAN HOUSE, SEAT OF DR. FARQUHARSON.

No. XVIII.—THE "KITH AND KIN" OF CLAN CHATTAN.

HAVING exhausted the authentic lists of the tribes as detailed by Sir Eneas Mackintosh, I finish this work with a brief account of those families known to have sprung from, or allied themselves with the Clan Chattan, more properly falling under the heading of the "Kith and Kin" of Clan Chattan.

They again may be divided into two branches—1st, those who dwelt in the county of Inverness, and 2nd, those settled in other counties; and they are placed alphabetically.

I.—Cattanach. This sept spread over Badenoch, but once important, are diminishing. The late Mr. James Cattanach, Kinlochlaggan, and the late Mr. Cattanach, Newtonmore, were both highly respected in their day.

II.—Crerar. This name of late is coming well to the front. Originally Mackintoshes, it is matter of tradition that the name took its rise in the person of a prominent member owing his safety to concealment from his foes in a manner somewhat similar to that connected with the Lobans of Drumderfit. Mr. Duncan Macgregor Crerar of New York, and Provost Crerar of Kingussie, with his promising son at present in Perth, are all zealous clansmen.

III.—Gillespie. This name is much scattered over Scotland, but many at different periods have adhered to Clan Chattan.

IV.—Gillies. Lachlan Mackintosh, 2nd son of Malcolm, 10th Mackintosh, married, according to the Kinrara History, "the daughter of the chieftain of the Clan Vic Gillies, that dwelt in Gaskmore, in Badenoch." The Gillies' of Badenoch were at one time numerous, but have almost died out. The name is at present very common in the Hebrides.

V.—Noble. This name was to be found chiefly in Strathnairn and Strathdearn, dwelling amid the Clan Chattan. Some—particularly tenants of Raigmore—are still to be found in the parish of Moy. Of the name I select three, each in different spheres showing a decided individuality, illustrating the name. (1)—Sir Andrew Noble, member of the great house of Armstrong & Co., Newcastle, of world-wide reputation; (2)—Mr. Noble, a native of Inverness, who, after a long service in the Cape of Good Hope, has now retired on a well-earned pension from the Parliament of that Colony; and (3)—my late worthy friend, Mr. John Noble, bookseller at Inverness, a most accomplished aider in building up the reputation of Inverness as a great centre for the disposal of Highland and Gaelic literature.

2.—THE FAMILIES IN ABERDEEN AND PERTH SHIRES.

At the head of these families falls to be placed

I.—MacHardies. This at one time influential name in Aberdeenshire and on the southern slopes of the Grampians, has of late begun to come well to the front, especially in the constabulary departments of Scotland. Histories have been written,—some with more zeal than discretion. That by Coghlan Maclean MacHardy, published in 1894, shows considerable research. There were at one time six landowners of the name in Perthshire, and the MacHardies, like the

Farquharsons, were greatly favoured by the Earls of Mar.

The MacHardies of Strathdon followed the banner of Mackintosh—those of Braemar that of the Farquharsons. Their lands were over-run by powerful neighbours, and it is noted that, in 1696, the fighting men of this once powerful tribe only numbered twenty-six.

Mr. Macbain, Rector of the High School of Inverness, suggests to me that the name may be derived from the Pictish "Gart Naigh," pronounced "Gratney," a well-known name of old in Mar. Mr. Macbain thinks that in time it changed to MacCardney or MacCarday—MacCartney in Irish—and ultimately, before 1587, to MacHardy. Mr. Macbain tells me what is very pertinent to this work, and I have much pleasure in recording, viz.—that the late Donald MacHardy of Daldownie, who died in 1870, descended from Duncan, who acquired Daldownie in 1710, informed him that claiming to be head of the MacHardies, "he owned no other chief than Mackintosh."

Much material has already been gathered connected with the MacHardies, but it is not open to the public; and there is a wide field to any enterprising historian to deal with the matter in an authentic form. No time should be lost, for numerous most interesting traditions connected with Corgarff, Cairn-na-Cuinne, and other localities, presently within reach, are, from the changed mode of possession, in danger of being lost.

II.—MacOmie. They are descended from a younger son of the 6th Mackintosh, and long held an influential position in Glenshee. To the Farquharson bond of 1594, granted to

Mackintosh as their chief, Robert MacOmie, in the burn of Glenshee, and Duncan Mackintosh, of Dalmunzie, are parties. In 1594, the above Robert Mackintosh is mentioned, also the name of Barbara Rattray, his wife, and Elizabeth MacOmie, his only daughter. In 1595, Elizabeth, with Duncan Mackintosh, alias MacRichie, in Dalmunzie, Lachlan Farquharson, in Bronchdearg, and others, her tutors, pay up in a formal manner on the 26th January, at Strath Ardill Kirk, a debt of 100 merks Scots, due by the late Robert MacOmie. Mr. MacCombie Smith has written a very interesting account of the MacOmies of Glenshee, of which family descended the late Mr. MacCombie, M.P., and Mr. MacCombie, of Easter Skene, also the well-known Vice-Admiral of Orkney, Sheriff Thoms.

Mr. Alexander MacOmie, in Glenshee, was, in 1693, one of the patriotic protesters against the English opponents of the Scots Darien Scheme; and was father of Elizabeth MacOmie, whom the Rev. Lachlan Shaw mentions as wife of Captain Duncan Mackintosh, 3rd son of the third Borlum. Being my great-great-grand parents, I must be excused from noticing that with the bride came from Glenshee to Inverness, some of her name, who settled chiefly in the heights of Borlum, in the Feabui now called Drumashie; and of them descended the MacOmies in Balnagaig of Dunain, the late Mr. Alexander Mackintosh, retired teacher, for many years resident at Culcabock, and others now named Mackintosh, but known amongst themselves and neighbours as MacOmies.

III.—Mackintoshes of Dalmunzie. They descend from Angus Oig, 3rd son of Angus, 6th Mackintosh. They removed to Perthshire, and since 1502 have been proprietors of Dalmunzie. Duncan Mackintosh, of Dalmunzie, is found as proprietor, and signs the Bond of Service to Mackintosh, as his chief, along with MacOmie of Glenshee, as formerly mentioned. Three generations bring us to John, who, in 1665, with three of his sons, appear supporting Mackintosh in the field in Badenoch and Lochaber. Two years later he supports his chief under the following circumstances :—

"In September, 1667, a party of Lochaber men came down to Glenisla, about the time Mackintosh had married Edzell's daughter, and took away a spreath of goods from Edzell's tenants. Mackintosh took this, as it was, a great affront, and resolved to repair Edzell's loss, or have full satisfaction from the actors. After a deal of time was lost, and with several crosses, he sets out for Lochaber, accompanied by Invercauld, Aberarder, Corrybrough Mor, Inverey, Nuid younger, Balnespick, Dalmunzie, the Tutor of Dunmaglass, and others in all, 300 able men—and marched from Garva, in Brae Badenoch, to Brae Lochaber, where his tenants of Glen Roy and Glen Spean, to the number of six score, meet him in good order; and, in December, kept his first Steward Court on the lands of Keppoch, and having gotten all due obedience in that place, thereafter caused restore the pre-mentioned spreath, which Huntly's tenants lately before had taken out of Glenisla."

It was on the above occasion that Mackintosh appealed to the Earl of Mar, hereditary friend of Mackintosh, who,

X

in reply, addressed to him the following letter, the spelling being partly modernized:—

"MUCH HONOURED COSEN,

In obedience to your intreaty, Sir, I have written to Invercauld, to take alongst with himself, my whole vassals and feuars in Braemar, Strath Dee and Glengairne to attend you, and accompany him in what you have to do in Loughaber. And as this is the best and most effectual order I can send them to make intimation hereof, as my will by Invercauld, who is my Bayliffe in this country, so shall I be ready, Sir, to witness my respects to you in a greater manner when occasion offers, Sir, your most affectionate cousin to serve you.

(Signed) J MAR.

TILLYFOUR, 26th November, 1667."

Addressed—

"For my much Honoured Cosen, the Laird of Mackintosh, these."

The Farquharsons, who accompanied Mackintosh in this expedition to Lochaber, included Invercauld, and Monaltrie from Aberdeenshire, and Mackintosh of Dalmunzie from Perthshire, and the prominent and valuable assistance given by the Farquharsons on that and other occasions is gratefully remembered to this day, and heartily acknowledged.

One of the family, Robert Mackintosh, advocate, was for some time Governor of the York Buildings Company; and a later member, Lachlan Mackintosh, was for many years editor of the *Morning Post*. The present representative is Mr. Charles Hills Mackintosh, who, though a resident in England, is an enthusiastic clansman, and justly proud of representing a family which, even two hundred years ago, the Kinrara historian describes as having "flourished a long time in great account and estimation."

IV.—The Toshes, or Toshachs, and MacGlashans, etc. The Toshes, the oldest cadets of the house of Mackintosh, breaking of before 1220, being descended of Edward, son of Shaw, 2nd Mackintosh, settled in Perthshire, and for a considerable period held a good position in Monzievaird, Culcreif, Pittenzie, and Glentilt.

In 1599, Lachlan Mackintosh of Mackintosh is entrusted by them—then sore pressed by powerful absorbing neighbours, the Drummonds of Perth and the Murrays of Athole—with the custody of their title deeds. This inventory, including some very ancient documents, came into my hands some years ago, at the cost of a few pence.

In 1450 Andrew Toshach grants the lands of Brewlands and others to the Monastery of Inchaffray. In 1502 Finlay Toshach is described as Thane of Glentilt, his lands extending to three davochs. In 1509 Andrew Toshach, upon his own resignation, gets a new grant of the free Barony of Monzievaird and free forestry of Glentorade. In 1596 Duncan Toshach of Pittenzie is mentioned, and as early as 1371 Eugenius, Thane of Glentilt. Connected with the Toshes or Toshachs were the old family called the sons of Adam, first Ayson, latterly Esson.

The MacGlashans, as well as the MacKerrachers, are considered to be of Clan Chattan.

APPENDIX.

I.—THE MACBEANS, page 56. The gallant services of Major Forbes Macbean at the taking of Dargai last October, which has conferred such honour upon the Gordon Highlanders, should not be omitted. It must be matter of high gratification to his father, Lieutenant-Colonel Forbes Macbean, formerly of the 92nd, to see the reputation of his family and his old regiment so brilliantly maintained, demonstrating that the spirit of Gillies Macbean, their kinsman of the "'45," exists in full strength. Major Macbean was severely wounded in the second battle of Dargai on 20th October, 1897, and has recently been promoted Brevet Lieut.-Colonel, and decorated with the Distinguished Service Order for his gallant conduct at this engagement. He married in 1889 Frances, daughter of the late Captain Fishbourne Jackson, R.N.

Of the clan was the late Rev. Mr. M'Vean, the respected and well-known minister of Iona. Like the minister of Inverness, Mr. M'Vean's descendants have become soldiers. The Rev. Mr. M'Vean's grandson is a Lieutenant in the 21st Punjaub Infantry, and served under General Jeffreys in his expedition connected with the Indian Frontier wars. Mr. C. A. M'Vean, father of the Lieutenant, is exerting himself in tracing out the family history, and the period when they adopted the present mode of spelling their surname.

II.—THE MACPHAILS, page 62. This paper attracted the notice, I am happy to say, of the head of the Macphails. Mr. Paul Macphail of Melbourne wrote to me under date of 16th November, 1897 :—

"It was with much interest I have read your memoirs of the Macphails of Inverairnie, which appeared in the July number of the *Celtic Monthly*. My interest in that article was enhanced, believing that I am the nearest surviving relative of the Inverairnie Macphails. My father, Donald Macphail, was a tenant in Balnuilt, Gask, under Dunmaglass, and was a son of Paul Macphail referred to by you, to whom Alexander Macphail executed a transfer of his estate on the 14th April, 1763. My father died when I was young, leaving a family of three. My brother Lachlan died in Inverness, 1882. My sister is still alive, and came to Australia in 1886. I am the eldest of our family, and came to Australia in 1852. Owing to our father's early death we know but little of family history. One part I can vouch for certainly, that Paul Macphail, to whom Alexander Macphail of Inverairnie assigned his estate in 1763, was my grandfather. I am not aware that my father had any brothers, but had a sister who survived him by many years. I regret I cannot give you more information in this matter."

In reply to my suggestion that he should assert his position and settle in his native district, Mr. Macphail says, that with every attachment to Strathnairn, yet being unmarried and somewhat advanced in life, he has accepted his adopted country, in which he has prospered, as his home.

As I have discovered the names of several Macphails in connection with Tullich and Elrig, prior to Duncan Macphail, given at page 59 as 1st of the family, I now append the note :—

1500—say Conchie dhu.
1546—Marion Fraser, daughter of Thomas Barron, otherwise

Thomas Ewen's son Fraser, grants to Duncan vic Conchie dhu in Inverairnie half of Tullich and Elrig.

1553—Paul vic Conchie dhu, heir of his father, Duncan vic Conchie dhu.

1557—Paul grants charter to his son, Duncan Macphail.

1582—Duncan Macphail is found.

1593—Duncan sells Tullich and Elrig to Lachlan Mac-Mackintosh of Mackintosh.

Page 62. Captain M'Fall has gone throughly into the family history, and his researches demand publication in separate and distinct form, for space prevents their being dealt with at present. Amidst other interesting matter, Captain M'Fall refers to Leyden's romantic ballad "Macphail of Colonsay" and "The Mermaid of Corryvreckan."

III.—MACQUEEN, page 63, line 7. For "centre" read "counties."

Page 82. A cherished piece of tartan was sent by an enthusiastic clanswoman, Miss Macqueen of Folkestone, daughter of Colonel Potter Macqueen and Jane Astley of Melton Constable. Her great-grandfather, a Skye man, fell at Culloden, whose son, Dr. Macqueen, removing to England, married the daughter of Dr. Potter, Archbishop of Canterbury, and they were the grand-parents of Miss Macqueen. Colonel Potter Macqueen was the first of the family born out of Scotland, where with pardonable pride Miss Macqueen mentions the family had been for nine hundred years.

IV.—SHAWS, page 91. As the preservation of ancient sayings

and rhymes is very important, I give the verses composed by an unfriendly bard and addressed to that Adam Shaw, in whose barn at Tordarroch the Earl of Moray caused so many to be slain, about the year 1530.

> "Adhamh mac Adhamh vic Adhamh riabhaich,
> Sàr biatiche na-h-Alba,
> Chunnaic mi do shabhull corca,
> Làn do chorpaibh marbha."

Which may be rendered—

> "Adam, son of Adam, son of Adam of the brandered countenance,
> The most choice and hospitable man in Scotland;
> I saw your barn for oats,
> Full of dead corpses."

Page 106. Mr. M. T. Shaw of Edinburgh has given me a good deal of information about the Aberdeenshire and Perthshire Shaws, and I have pleasure in giving this additional information, viz.:—That William Shaw of Dalnaglar, still remembered as "Factor Shaw," married in 1779 Margaret, daughter of John Robertson of Cray, by whom he had seven sons and two daughters. In 1787 he removed from Dalnaglar to Soilarzie, of which he had a twenty-one years' tack from the Duke of Athole, on the expiry of which he took the farm of Over Kinfauns, where he resided until his death.

V.—CLARKS—page 117. In the parish of Kirkhill, Inverness, Mr. John Paterson Clark was in this century proprietor of the estate of Fingask, while in the neighbouring parish of Kiltarlity, Colonel James Cumming Clarke of Ballindoun presently worthily represents the clan.

VI.—MACINTYRES. Mr. D. A. S. Mackintosh of Bertrohill House, Shettleston, that picturesque Highlander of the old school, and president of the Glasgow Association, of whom Clan Chattan may be proud, writes me in correction of the commonly received definition of the name as the "son of the wright." Mr. Mackintosh being of the Macintyres, both his grandmothers bearing that name, has looked into the question thoroughly, fortified by what was told him when a boy by his great-uncle, Neil Macintyre, and I cannot do better than give his own words:—

"Macdonald, called Cean-teire from his ownership of Kintyre, had a son called John, who acquired the lands of Degnish, a promontory lying between Loch Melford and Ardmaddy Loch, where is the Nether Lorne Castle of the Marquis of Breadalbane. His son John was called John Mac-Cein-teire-na-Dhegnish, from being the son of Canteire, and himself John of Degnish. My uncle could tell all the names downwards, from John to his own father, who was also called John. The descendants of this John Mac-Cean-teire-Dhegnish were alternatively called John and Donald.

Another branch of the Macintyres origined in the same way from a brother of the said John of Degnish, who was called Donald, and acquired lands at Ben Cruachan, Loch Awe. His son was called Mac-Cein-tyre Cruachan, and in this way came the name of Macintyre to light."

The above derivation of the name of Macintyre from the great district of Kintyre should gratify all of the name, and they have good reason to thank the gigantic Highlander of their kin, through whom, it is to be hoped, the matter may now be held as finally settled.

VII.—MACANDREWS, page 143. The names of the following two members of the clan should not be overlooked:—

(1) Mr. William Macandrew, who, after an active commercial career abroad has settled in Essex, restored in 1888 the old Market Cross of Elgin, the place of his birth.

(2) Captain John Maclean Macandrew, who has restored the old castle of Dalcross, an interesting historic place in the parish of Croy, combining with an harmonious preservation of the past, all the comforts of present day occupation. The situation of the castle is one of the most commanding in the North.

VIII.—DAVIDSONS. I omitted to mention that the last of the Davidsons of Invernahaven changed his name about the end of the seventeenth century to Macpherson. This was strange, considering the antagonistic position of old assumed by David dhu. A possible explanation is the fact that by this time Invernahaven and most of the surrounding district was owned by the Macphersons.

Davidson of Tulloch mentions that his predecessors were recognized as heads of the Clan, and that he is presently acknowledged to be chieftain.

Absence from Scotland, however long, does not often diminish Scottish love of family and country. Mr. Thomas Davidson (of West Hampstead), together with his father and grand-father have been settled in England; but he does not forget that his great-great-grandfather, James, with a brother, Dunbar Davidson, both fought and fell at Culloden. Mr. Davidson's predecessors were Lowland Scots from the neighbourhood of Kelso, at Yetholm, Roxburghshire. One of the family was the unfortunate William Davison, secretary to Queen Elizabeth.

Amongst the family relics in Mr. Davidson's possession—published in Howard's "Miscellanea Genealogica et Heraldica,"—are the original Grant of Arms to William Davison, the broadsword, dirk, and pistols, of Captain Alexander Davidson, presumed to be a brother of James, and who also fell at Culloden. Thus it will be seen that the three brothers—James, Dunbar, and Alexander Davidson, were all killed on the same unhappy day.

BOND OF UNION BY AND BETWIXT THE TRIBES OF CLAN CHATTAN, 1609.

At Termett the 4th day of April the year of God 1609, It is appointed Bonded Contracted concorded finally ended and agreed betwixt the Honourable persons and parties as follows vizt. William Mackintosh of Banchar as Principal Captain of the haill kin of Clan Chattan as having the full place thereof for the present induring the minority of Lachlan Mackintosh of Dunachton his Brother's son, for himself and taking the full burden in and upon him of Malcolm Mackintosh of Urlust and remanent of his brethren with their own consent under subscribing; Angus Mackintosh of Termett for himself and takan the burden in and upon him of Lachlan Mackintosh his son apparent thereof with his own consent, and assent of his remanent sons under subscribing, Lachlan Mackintosh of Gask for himself and taking the burden in and upon him of William Mackintosh of Rait and remanent of that surname descended of that house with their own consent under subscribing; Andrew Macpherson of Cluny for himself and taking the full burden in and upon him of Evan Macpherson in Brin, John Macpherson in Breakachy, with their own consent and remanent of that name descended from and of that house; Thomas vic Allister vic Thomas in Pitmean and taking full burden in and upon him of his kin and friends descended of his house; Donald Macallister Roy in Phones for himself and taking full burden in and upon him of William M'Ian vic William in Invereshie with his own consent and remanent his kin of that race and house; Donald M'Queen of Corrybrough for himself and taking full burden in and upon him of John M'Queen in Little Corriburgh, Sween M'Queen in Raigbeg, with their own consent and remanent his kin of that race; Angus M'Pol in Kinchyle for himself and takand the full burden in and upon him of his kin and race of Clan Vean; Alexander MacCoil vic Farquhar of Davoch Garioch for himself and takand the full burden in and upon him of his kin and race of Clan Tarlaich with their own consents; Malcolm MacBean in Dalcrombie Ewen M'Ewen in Aberchalder and Duncan M'Farquhar in Dunmaglass for themselves and takand the full

burden in and upon them of their haill kin and race of Clan Vic-Gillvray with their own consents: and Ay MacBean vic Robt. of Tordarroch for himself and takand the full burden in and upon him of his race of Clan Ay with their own consents, in manner form and effects as after follows: That is to say that for as meikle as anent the controversies questions and debates and hosts that has fallen furth betwixt the said haill kin of Clan Chattan these times byegone whereupon there followed great inconveniences committed by them one against the other without any respect of their own weals coming thereof, and for avoiding of these accidents, and that perpetual friendship amity and kindness may remain and abide betwixt them and their Chief in times coming, and amongst the said haill kin of Clan Chattan. Therefore and for sundry other motives and occasions moving them tending to the weals and quietness of them and their country, are hereby bound and obliged, and by the tenour hereof the said haill kin of Clan Chattan above mentioned by their names in special and takand full burden in and upon them of their kin and friends airs and partakers *pro rato*, faithfully promise and bind and oblige them by the faith and truth in their bodies for themselves with consent foresaid their heirs male and successours, to the said William Mackintosh their present Captain and Chief, aye and while the said Lachlan Mackintosh of Dunachton comes to manhood and perfect age (and then to him) to concur assist maintain and defend against all other and whatsoever persons that shall happen to invade him, and to be found loyal upright and true to him in all his honest and lessom affairs whatsoever: Like as they to that effect, has united incorporat annex copulate and insinuat themselves in one bond and perpetual amity to stand amongst them as it was of auld according to the King of Scotlands gift of Chieftainrie of the said Clan Chattan granted thereupon, in the which they are and is astricted to serve Mackintosh as their Captain and Chief. Therefore the saids haill persons of chief and kin Clan Chattan, bind and oblige them ilk ane of them to others the said William and the said kin of Clan Chattan, to concur assist maintain and defend either others, or to take plain art and part with others, against all and whatsoever persons in all actions of arms deeds and occasions whatsoever that shall happen to be done in their contrair or that shall happen to fall furth thereafter, the Kings Grace the

Lord Marquis of Huntly and the Earl of Moray (their masters) being excepted, providing that it be in their Lords and masters default in case any deed or host fall out be their occasions ; And also the haill kin of Clan Chattan has discharged and quit claimed and be the tenour hereof quit claims and exoners and simpliciter discharges either others and ilk one of them of all actions of slaughter burning hership raid and oppression committed by them or any of them against others preceding the day and date hereof discharging the same and all action that may result thereupon ; And that all rancour and malice of heart for ever and also in case any of the saids kin shall happen to offend any other in time coming either by violence or avenge of gear, in that case the Chief shall nominate twelve persons of the said principals to decide with him therein and shall cause the party offended and wronged such as they will decern and modify ; and to the haill premises the said Chief and remanent kin of Clan Chattan are sworn to stand at and perform the points above mentioned and never to revoke or come in the contrar thereafter, but shall maintain and pass ilk one of them with others in all hostings and other lessom and necessary affairs as when occasions will serve (excepting as excepted). And for the more security the said William Mackintosh and remanent his kin of Clan Chattan are content and consents that these presents be insert in the Books of Council and Session, Sheriff, or Commissary, Burgh Court Books of Inverness there to remain *ad futuram rei memoriam* and to that effect constitutes and ordains. Procurators conjunctly and severally and consents to the registration hereof *promitten de rato*. In witness whereof these presents written by Alexander Duff Notary Public and Common Clerk of Inverness, are subscribed by the said Chief and kin day year and place foresaid, before these witnesses John Cuthbert of Auldcastlehill Provost of Inverness, Mr. John Ross Burgess there, Donald Macqueen Minister of Petty, Malcolm Ego Servitor to Agnes Mackenzie Lady Dunachton and Alexander Duff Writer hereof.

   (Signed) WILLIAM MACKINTOSH OF BEANDACHAR,
       Captain of Clan Chattan.
    MALCOLM MACKINTOSH (Captain's Brother).
    LACHLAN MACKINTOSH OF GASK.

(Signed) LACHLAN MACKINTOSH, APPARENT OF
TERMITT.
ANDREW MAKFERSONE OF CLUNY.
EWEN MACPHERSON OF BRIN.
JOHN MACPHERSON IN BREACKACHIE.
DONALD MACQUEEN OF CORRYBROUGH.
AY MACBEAN OF TORDARROCH.
WM. MACKINTOSH IN RAIT.
JOHN MACKINTOSH OF DALZIEL.
DUNCAN MACKINTOSH (CAPTAIN'S BROTHER).
GILLIE CALLUM MACKINTOSH IN OVY.

Angus Mackintosh of Termitt, Thomas MacAllister vic Thomas in Pitmain, Angus MacPhail in Kinchyle, Alexander Mackintosh of the Holm, Alexander Mackintosh, Hector's son in Wester Leys, Donald MacAllister Roy in Foiness, with our hands at the pen, led by the Nottar at our command, because we cannot write ourselves.

Ita est Alexander Duff, Notarius Publicus admissus praemissa subscribere, de mandato dict personarum scribere nescien in fide requisitus teste manu propria.

John Mackintosh, Angus' son in Morill, Alexander Mac Coil vic Farquhar in Dochgarroch, Malcolm Mac Bean in Dalcrombie, Sween Macqueen in Raige, John Mac Iain dhu vic Coil vic Neill in Strathmashie, Alexander Mac Farquhar vic Thomas, John dhu Mac Coil Vor, our hands led at the pen by Alexander Duff, Nottar, because we cannot write.

Ita est Alexander Duff, Notarius Publicus admissus praemissa subscribere, de mandato dict personarum scribere nescien in fide requisitus teste manu propria.

(Signed) JOHN CUTHBERT OF YE AULDCASTLEHILL,
Witness.
MR. JOHN ROSS, Witness.
MALCOLM EGO, Witness.

(From a notarial copy of the Bond made and subscribed at Borlum,
27th March, 1724.)

DEED OF 1664.

We under subscribing gentlemen of the name of Clan Chattan, (in obedience to His Majesty's authority, and Letters of Concurrence granted by the Lords of Council of His Majesty's Privy Council, in favour of Lachlan Mackintosh of Torcastle (our Chieffe) against Evan Cameron of Lochzield, and certain others of the name of Clan Cameron, and for the love and favour we have to the said Lachlan, do hereby faithfully promise and engage ourselves (everyone of us for himself and those under his power) in case the pre-mentionat Evan Cameron (and those of his kin now rebels) do not agree with the said Lachlan anent the present differs and controversies, before the third day of February next to come, that then and in that case shall immediately thereafter upon the said Lachlan his call) rise with, fortify, concur and assist the said Lachlan in the prosecution of the commission granted against the said Evan to the uttermost of our power, with all those of our respective friends, followers, and dependents whom we may stop or lett, or who in any way will be compelled and advised by us to that effect. And hereto we faithfully engage ourselves upon our reputation and credit, and the faith and truth in our bodies: By these subscribed at Kincairne the nineteent day of November and year of God Sixteen Hundred and Sixty-four years.

    (Signed) JOHN MACPHERSON OF BRIN.
             THOMAS M'CONCHIE ROY. × his sign.
             JO. MACPHERSON OF INNERESSIE.
             JOHN MACPHERSON, T. (Tutor of Invereshie).
             DONALD MACPHERSON OF PHONESS.
             MURDO MACPHERSON OF DRUMINORD.
             EVAN MACPHERSON OF PITGOUN.
             MURDO MACPHERSON OF CLUNE.
             THOMAS MACPHERSON.
             FARQUHAR MACGILLIVRAY OF DUNMAGLASS.
             A. MACKINTOSH IN DALNACRASK.

Wee undersubscryvit and Gentlemen of the Name of Clanchattan (In obedience
to his Majesties authority, & Letters of Concurrence granted be the Lords
of his Ma:ties publict counsell, In favours of Lauchlan Mackintoshe of
Torcastle (our Chieffe) against Ewen Cameron of Lochyeill (and certain
others of the name of Clanchameron, and for the Love and favour
wee beare to thir N. Lauchlan Doe hereby faithfullie promitt, Ingadge
ourselfes (ilkain ane of us for himself & thair aires & co posteritie) wt ye said
the afornamed Ewen Cameron (and such of his nae rebells of Lochaber
aires wt the said Lauchlan anent this present Differens and controversie
befor the first ____ Day of Febrwary nixtocum thairefter and in the caise
____ the said Lauchlan his call) shall
assist wt, fortifie concurre, and assist the said Lauchlan in the
prosecution of the Comission granted against the said Ewen to the
uttermost of our power, They all this or any refusal faile followard, &
depriued whom wee may from a Lott or in the will in any way be compelled
the absyde the said to ffect And thirto this faithfull Ingadgem:t
ourselfes upon our reputatione and credite, wee testifie sub: manu
in token thereof By this subscribed at Inverness this nynteint day
of Nov:ber and yeire of God [16]hundreth and four ____

Jon M: person of Cuchin

[multiple signatures:]
J. M:pherson of ...
John M:pherson ... James M:pherson ...
Ewen M: pherson ... M:intoshe of Clune
of Pronot
nod M:pherson of Dumnaie
Dow M: Jondon Pitpoan
angus m: gilivre
Anns ffragon ... Robert Reall
Ewnes m: pherson ... Donald m: Keoir m:ffula
Pat:k M: gillivray ... Donald M:gillivray tutor of Dunach:
of Dunaglass ... William M: gilivray in Borgs
F. M:intoshe in Drumcrosk

APPENDIX.

(Signed) WM. MACKINTOSH OF KELACHIE.
JAMES MACKINTOISHE.
LACHLAN MACKINTOSH OF ABERARDER.
JOHN MACKINTOSH OF DELMIGAVIE.
W. McK.
PAUL MACBEAN OF KINCHYLE.
ROBERT SHAW (7th OF TORDARROCH).
J. FARQUHARSON OF INVEREY.
CHARLES FARQUHARSON OF MONALTRIE.
JA. FARQUHARSON OF WHITEHOUSE, Your.
J. SHAW (OF DELL).
GEO. FARQUHARSON (BROUCHDEARG).
ANGUS MACQUEEN (2nd OF CORRYBROUGH.
A. McB.
DONALD MACBEAN OF FAILLIE.
DONALD MACGILLIVRAY, Tutor of Dunmaglass.
WILLIAM MACGILLIVRAY IN LARGS.

CONSENT, APPROVAL, AND REQUEST BY THE CLAN CHATTAN, 1756.

INDEX.

Alasdair Ciar, ...	86, 147
Alastair Ruadh na Feille, ...	15
Allargue and Breda, Farquharson of,	169
Angusius Haraldi, ...	141
Andrew, Sir W. P., ...	143
Ardclach, Macbeans of, ...	56
Assynt, Parson at, ...	64
Battle of North Inch, Perth, ...	84, 118, 120, 123
Bodach an Dùin, ...	111
Bond of Union by and betwixt the tribes of Clan Chattan,	188
Braxfield, Macqueen of, ...	74
Camerons, Bond of Union against the,	192
Camerons at Culloden, ...	19
Campbell of Clunes, Sir Archibald, ...	17
Campbell of Clunes, Duncan, ...	17
Campbell of Clunes, Miss Elizabeth—interesting letter, ...	18
Captain Bàn, The, ...	10
Cattanach, ...	173
Clan an t-Saoir, or Macintyres of Badenoch, ...	136-138, 185
Clan Ay, ...	90, 91, 103, 127
Clan Cay, ...	118
Clan Chattan Association, ...	128
Clan Chattan Confederation—Bond of 1609, 4—Text of Bond, 8,	144, 188
Clan Dhai, or Davidson, ...	123, 127, 186
Clan Dhu of Strathnairn, ...	145
Clan Finlay Cheir, ...	145
Clan Finnlay, or Farquharson, ...	147, 193
Clan Maclean Association, ...	135
Clan Quele, ...	118
Clan Tarrill, ...	139
Clan Thearlaich (Macleans), ...	129, 188

THE CLARKS,	... 112-117, 183
Clark, Rev. Alexander,	... 115
Clark, Sir Andrew, (1456),	 114
Clark, Sir Thomas, ...	 117
Clarks, Materials for History, ...	 114
Clarks, six Baronets of name,	 117
Corrybrough, Macqueens of,	 63
Crerar, ...	 173
Crerar, Duncan Macgregor,	 173
Crerar, Provost, Kingussie,	 173
Culloden, ...	15, 19, 34, 80, 182, 186
Culloden Relics, ...	... 108, 109, 186
THE DAVIDSONS, OR CLAN DHAI,	... 123-128, 185
Daars, Macbeans of, ...	 39-42
Dalnavert, Shaws of,	 101
Deed of 1664, — ...	... 192
Dell, Shaws of, ...	... 97-98
Dochgarroch, Macleans of,	... 129-135, 188
Drummond, Macbeans of,	... 36-39
Duart, Maclean of, ...	... 129-135
Duke of Tarentum, ...	 107
Dunmaglass, Macgillivrays of, ...	2, 9, 13, 28, 192
THE FARQUHARSONS, ...	147-172
I.—Farquharsons of Inverie, ...	... 161
II.—Farquharsons of Monaltrie, ...	... 162
III.—Farquharsons of Whitehouse, ...	... 163
IV.—Farquharsons of Haughton, ...	... 167
V.—Farquharsons of Allargue and Breda, ..	... 169
VI.—Farquharsons of Finzean, ...	... 170
Farquharsons, called Clann Fhinnlay, ...	147, 193
Farquharsons at Culloden, ...	153-155
Farquharson, "Colonel Anne,"	153
Farquharsons descended from Finlay More, 1547,	147
Farquharson, Robert, of Invercauld, ...	150
Faillie, Macbeans of, ...	42

Fairy Tale, A, (The Captain Bàn), ...	10
Findlay Mor (Farquharson),	147
Finzean, Farquharson of, ...	150
Forbes, Duncan, of Culloden,	6
Forbes of Skellater, ...	6
Fraser, Donald, (Captain of Five),	71, 78, 82
Fraser of Balnain,	14
Gillespie, ...	173
Gillies, ...	173
Gorries, Vic, ...	144
THE GOWS (SLIOCHD GOW CROM), ...	118-122
Gaelic Toasts, ...	55
"Governor Shaw,"	94
Gowie, John, ...	122
Hal o' the Wynd, ...	118
Haughton, Farquharsons of,	167
Inverairnie, Macphails of,	57-62, 181
Invercauld, Farquharsons of, ...	149-152
Inverie, Farquharsons of,	161
Invernahaven, Battle of,	125
THE "KITH AND KIN" OF CLAN CHATTAN,	173-179
Families in the County of Inverness—	
I.—Cattanach, ...	173
II.—Crerar, ...	173
III.—Gillespie, ...	173
IV.—Gillies, ...	173
V.—Noble, ...	174
Families in Aberdeen and Perth Shires—	
I.—MacHardies, ...	174
II —MacOmie, ...	175
III.—Mackintoshes of Dalmunzie, ...	177
IV.—Toshes, or Toshachs, and MacGlashans,	179
THE MACANDREWS, ...	142-143, 184
MacAndrews, or Gillandrish, Origin of Name,	 142

MacAndrew, John Beg, celebrated bowman, 143
MacAndrew, Donald, Bridge of Dulsie, ... 143
MacAndrew, Sir Henry C., ... 163
MacAndrew, Captain J. Maclean, ... 186
MacAndrew, William, ... 186
  MACBEANS OF KINCHYLE, 31-36, 180, 193
I.—Angus, (1610), ... 31
II.—John, (1628), ... 33
III.—Paul, (1664), ... 33, 193
IV.—William, (1686), ... 33
V.—Eneas, (1711), ... 34
VI.—Gillies, (1745), 34, 180
VII.—Donald, (1751), ... 35
  MACBEANS OF DRUMMOND, ... 36-39
  MACBEANS OF DAARS, PART OF KINCHYLE, ... 39-42
  MACBEANS OF FAILLIE, ... 42-49, 193
I.—Donald, (1632), ... 42
II.—Donald, (1661), ... 44, 193
III.—Donald, (1707), ... 45
IV.—William, (1749), 45
V.—Donald, (1768), ... 48
  MACBEANS OF TOMATIN, ... 49-56
I.—Bean, (1639), ... 51
II.—Eugenius or Evan, (1677), 51
III.—John, (1688), ... 51
IV.—William, (1742), 52
V.—Ludovic, (1760), ... 53
VI.—William, (1822), ... 54
VII.—Duncan, (1851), ... 54
VIII.—Ludovic, (1854), 54
IX.—William, (1879), 54
X.—Lachlan, (1883), .. 55
Macbean, Rev. Alexander, 40
Macbean, Rev. Angus, ... 40
Macbeans, Deed by, 1721, 38
Macbean, Eneas, ... 56

INDEX.

Macbean, Major-General,	56
Macbean, Gillies, at Culloden,	34
Macbean, Sir James, ...	56
Macbeans, Origin of,	30
Macbean Territory,	30
MacComies, ...	106
Macdonalds at Culloden, ...	19
Macdonald, Marshal, ...	107
MacFall, Captain Crawford,	182
MACGILLIVRAYS OF DUNMAGLASS, ...	1-29, 192
I.—Duncan, (1500), ...	3, 4
II.—Farquhar, (1547), ...	4
III.—Allister Mor, (1578), ...	4
IV.—Farquhar, (1620), ...	4
V.—Allister, (1654), ...	6
VI.—Farquhar Fiadhaich, (1658), ...	9
VII.—Farquhar, (1714), ...	13
VIII.—Alexander, Allister Ruadh na Feille, (1745), ...	15
IX.—William, (1779), ...	19
X.—John Lachlan, (1800), ...	21
XI.—Hon. John, (1852), ...	27
XII.—Neil John, (1855), ...	27
XIII.—J. W. MacGillivray, (1897), ...	28
MacGillivray, Origin of Name, ...	2
MacGillivray Lands, ...	5
MacGillivray, Bean, of Dalcrombie, ...	4
MacGillivray, Malcolm, ...	4
MacGillivray, Martin, of Aberchalder, ...	6
MacGillivray, Rev. Lachlan, ...	7, 26
MacGillivray, Captain William, ...	11, 27
MacGillivray, Part taken in risings of 1715 and 1745,	13, 15, 19
MacGillivray Place of Sepulture, ...	15
MacGillivray, Lachlan Liath, ...	10, 22, 27
MacGillivray Rent roll in 1803, ...	22-25
MacGlashans,	179

MacHardies,	174
MACINTYRES OF BADENOCH,	136-138, 185
MacIntyre, otherwise Clan Intoir or Clann an t-Saoir,	136
MacIntyre, Bard,	136
MacIntyre, Lieutenant-General John,	137
MacIntyre, E. J., Q. C.,	138
MacIntyre, Duncan Bàn,	138
MacIntyre, Dr., Kilmonivaig,	138
MacIntyre, Miss Margaret,	138
MacIntyre, Rev. Donald,	138
MacIntyres of Gleno,	137
Macintyre, Derivation of Name,	184
Mackerrachers,	179
Mackintosh, Hector,	8
Mackintosh, Largs,	10
Mackintoshes at Culloden,	19
Mackintosh, Provost of Inverness, 1779,	20
Mackintosh, Eva,	30, 31
Mackintosh's Lament,	136, 137
Mackintoshes of Dalmunzie,	177
Mackintoshes,	188-192
MACLEANS OF THE NORTH,	129-135
I. Sir Charles Maclean,	129
II.—Hector,	131
III.—Farquhar Gorach,	131
IV.—Donald,	132
V. Alexander, (1609),	132
VI. John, (1674),	133
VII.—Alexander, (1671),	133
VIII. John, (1682),	133
IX.—John, (1710),	133
X.—Charles, (1752),	133
XI.—John, (1826),	134
XII.—William, (1841),	134
XIII.—Allan,	135

XIV.—William, ...	135
XV.—Allan, ...	... 135
Maclean, Clan Association,	... 135
Macleans, Clan Thearlaich,	129-135
MacOmies, ...	175

THE MACPHAILS OF INVERAIRNIE,   57-62, 181

I.—Duncan, (1631), ...	59
II.—Paul, (1689),	59
III.—Robert, (1721), ...	60
IV.—Alexander, (1756),	60
Macphail, Gillies,	58
Macphail Lands,	59
Macphail, Origin of Name, ...	... 57, 62
Macphail, Rev. Andrew, (1594), ...	58
Macphail, written M'Faill, Phoil, Pol,	62
Macphail, Paul, Melbourne, ...	181
Macphersons,	125, 126, 144, 188, 191, 192

THE MACQUEENS.   ... 63-76 182, 188, 193

I.—Donald, (1594), ...	69, 191
II.—Angus, (1632),	69, 193
III.—Donald, (1676),	69
IV.—Donald, (1685),	70
V.—James, (1711),	70
VI.—Donald, (1740),	70
VII—Donald, (1758),	71
VIII.—Donald, (1815),	74
IX.—John Fraser, (1838),	74
X.—Lachlan, (1896), ...	75
XI.—Donald, (1898), ...	76

THE MACQUEENS OF POLLOCHAIG, CLUNE, STRATHNOON,   77-82

Macqueens, called Clan Revan, ...	63
Macqueen, Captain Donald, ...	73
Macqueen, Colonel Potter, ...	182
Macqueen, "Parson of Petty".	68
Macqueen Possessions,	73

Macqueen, Sir John Withers, K.C.B.,	82
Macqueen Tartan, ...	182
Macqueen, William, Sub-Dean of Ross,	... 64-68
MacVeans,	180
Nobles, ...	174
O'Clery, ...	113
Parson of Assynt, ...	64
Pollochaig, Macqueens of,	... 77-82
Prince Charlie Relics, ...	108-109
THE SHAWS OF ROTHIEMURCHUS,	... 83-89
I. Shaw Mackintosh, (1396), ...	... 84
II. James, (1411), ...	... 86
III.—Alasdair Ciar, (1464),	86
IV. John, ...	87
V.—Allan, (1536),	87
VI. James, ...	... 87
THE SHAWS OF TORDARROCH,	89-97, 182
I. Angus, (1468),	... 90
II.—Robert, ...	... 91
III. Angus, (1543), ...	91
IV.—Bean or Benjamin,	... 91
V. Adam, (1609),	... 91
VI. Angus, (1622),	... 92
VII.—Robert, (1666), ...	... 92
VIII. Alexander, (1679),	... 93
IX.—Angus, (1717), ...	... 93
X. Alexander, (1790), ...	... 94
XI. John, Major-General, (1835),	... 94
XII. John Andrew, (1842), ...	... 95
XIII. Charles Forbes, (1897),	... 95-97
THE SHAWS OF DELL, ...	... 97-98
I.—Alasdair Og, ...	... 97
II.—James, ...	... 97
III.—Alasdair, ...	... 97
IV.—Alasdair Og,	... 97

INDEX.

V.—John,	97
VI.—John,	98, 193
VII. Alexander, (1681),	98
VIII. James, (1758),	98
THE SHAWS OF DALNAVERT,	101
THE SHAWS OF KINRARA,	102
THE SHAWS, OR M'AYS, OF THE BLACK ISLE,	103, 189
THE SHAWS OF ABERDEEN, PERTH, AND THE ISLES,	104-110, 183
I. Allister Roy,	104
II.—James,	104
III.—James,	104
IV.—Duncan, (1726),	104
V.—Duncan,	106
VI. William,	106
VII.—Duncan, (1810),	107
VIII. Charles, (1885),	107
IX.—Duncan, (1889),	108
Shaws in America,	111
Shaws in Ireland,	110
Shaws' Motto:—"Fide et Fortitudine,"	111
Shaw, Rev. Lachlan,	57, 63, 99
Sibbald, Sir Robert,	97
Sliochd Gille vor Mac Aonas,	145
THE CLAN TARILL,	139
Tarill, Andrew, (1457),	139
Tarill Burying-Place,	141
Tarill, Meaning of Name,	141
Tomatin, Macbeans of,	49
Toshes or Toshachs,	179
Vic Gorries,	144
Whitehouse, Farquharsons of,	163
Witness burned alive for perjury,	10

www.ingramcontent.com/pod-product-compliance
Lightning Source LLC
Chambersburg PA
CBHW031733230426
43669CB00007B/340